IMAGES
of America
CHALDEAN IRAQI
AMERICAN ASSOCIATION
OF MICHIGAN

IMAGES
of America

CHALDEAN IRAQI AMERICAN ASSOCIATION OF MICHIGAN

Jacob Bacall

ARCADIA
PUBLISHING

Copyright © 2018 by Jacob Bacall
ISBN 978-1-4671-2762-2

Published by Arcadia Publishing
Charleston, South Carolina

Printed in the United States of America

Library of Congress Control Number: 2018930632

For all general information, please contact Arcadia Publishing:
Telephone 843-853-2070
Fax 843-853-0044
E-mail sales@arcadiapublishing.com
For customer service and orders:
Toll-Free 1-888-313-2665

Visit us on the Internet at www.arcadiapublishing.com

I dedicate this book to the early Chaldean immigrants who first set foot in this blessed land of America. Without them knowing, their choice of Detroit, Michigan, would change the history of Chaldean habitat forever. Now, this Great Lakes state has the largest Chaldean concentration in the world, including our country of origin, Mesopotamia, now Iraq.

One hundred percent of the author's proceeds and royalties from this book will be donated to the Chaldean Cultural Center in West Bloomfield, Michigan, a 501(c)(3) federally tax-exempt organization.

CONTENTS

FOREWORD

Founded in 1943, the Chaldean Iraqi American Association of Michigan (CIAAM), hailed by Jacob Bacall as the "mother of all organizations," is celebrating its 75th anniversary. After many failed attempts to spark the start of this group, CIAAM now stands strong, having weathered three quarters of a century in an ever-changing landscape and currently boasting a roster of more than 900 active member families. Operating in the Shenandoah Country Club, CIAAM has been dedicated to preserving the Chaldean culture and is home to the first Chaldean museum in the world.

Every picture in this book tells a story, and every story includes a historical image that gives a true sense of life at that moment in time.

In its infant stages, CIAAM worked tirelessly for many years before members were able to purchase a mere four acres in Southfield, Michigan, where the very first clubhouse—appropriately dubbed the Southfield Manor—was erected. The Southfield Manor transitioned slowly into what we know today as Shenandoah Country Club in West Bloomfield. Both of these clubs stood as testaments to the success of Chaldeans who migrated to Detroit from Iraq.

Shenandoah Country Club allows Chaldeans from all around Southeast Michigan to have a space all their own while simultaneously engaging within the communities they now call home. From social gatherings to over-the-top lavish Chaldean weddings, community affairs, and family celebrations, Shenandoah is the perfect example of the successes and contributions Chaldeans are making in Southeast Michigan.

Having immigrated to Michigan in 1977, Jacob Bacall served in every position on the CIAAM board over the last 30 years. There is no one better to write about CIAAM and its accomplishments; Jacob perfectly encapsulates what we know to be a successful Chaldean American, drawing from his own experiences and personal insights.

In this book, his follow-up to 2014's *Chaldeans in Detroit*, Jacob dives deeper into Michigan's Chaldean community, focusing on one of the most pivotal Chaldean organizations of our time. From the rough stages of CIAAM's inception to the 147 acres on which Shenandoah comfortably sits today, this book will serve to remind each and every one of us where we started as a community and how much further we can advance.

—Martin Manna
President
Chaldean American Chamber of Commerce

ACKNOWLEDGMENTS

I would like to start by thanking everyone who has helped me to learn what I did not know. Many of my friends and fellow club members enriched me with their insight, assistance, and patience. I have to admit that I've learned to listen more than I talk.

A word of appreciation goes first to those who left their home village of Telkaif and chose America to be their home for many generations to come. Those who planted the seeds of immigration turned out to be the "Rock of Simon" on which the Chaldeans built their new home and adopted a new country. I am appreciative to those who have shared their photographs or valuable stories and those who offered their support and encouragement to write this history of the first Chaldean association in America.

I would like to thank Dr. John Kassid for being the number-one motivator behind the writing of this book; Martin Manna for his continued support; my cousin Michael Sarafa for his encouragement and guidance; Terri Shammami, a dedicated motherly employee serving CIAAM since the 1980s; and Natasha Kuza, Clair Konja, John Oram, Junior Jwad, and Ralph Ayar for being great sources of information. Special thanks to Mary Romaya, Raad Kathawa, and Francis Boji for their continued support and follow up. Shenandoah's general manager and top chef, Lee Sharkas, your efforts were greatly appreciated. I would also like to extend my gratitude to those who provided images and valuable information to complete this book: Faris Nalu, Nabby Yono, *wishliani* champion Fakhri Garmo, Sharkey Haddad, Rodney George, Doug Saroki, Dr. Talat Karmo, my good friend Burt Kassab, Julie Hakim, Rosemary Bannon, and her sweetheart of a daughter, Contessa. Najiba Ayar Shouneyia and Saher, Cesar, and Nicole Yaldo, thank you very much. I am grateful to Faisal Arabo for his assistance. I would also like to thank Joyce Wiswell for her editorial help. Last but not least, thanks to Mayor Gerald Naftaly, David Flaisher, West Bloomfield supervisor Stephen Kaplan, Vanessa Denha Garmo, and Lisa Kalou.

A special thank-you to my wife, Anne, for letting me get away with disrupting our family weekend plans for months while I was busy writing this book, and to my sons, Mark and Joseph, who filled my absence at work when I needed it. I am grateful to the efforts of the mother of my three granddaughters, Simone, Aubrey, and Carmen—Christina is a daughter every father wishes to have. Without her help, it would have been nearly impossible to write this book. To her husband, Saifee, thank you. I am appreciative of my other daughter, Caroline, who was my right hand for my first book, *Chaldeans in Detroit*, and lent a hand with this book as well.

For those who are not mentioned but were essential players in my search for history finding its way into this book, a heartfelt thanks to you all.

INTRODUCTION

This book was written to preserve history and inspire others to be involved and engaged with their community for the well-being of the majority. "History is the record of the institution in good times and bad; written down, it is a document of character," said Joseph M. Dodge, Detroit Bank and Trust chairman.

A considerable amount of time, tremendous effort, and a great degree of interest were put into this book. But to describe the Chaldean experience, one had to serve and come to know it first-hand. Every attempt has been made to verify the information herein, but we are human and do not claim to be perfect. I spent a considerable amount of time interviewing and listening to the stories of these pioneers' lives, which were full of the experience and excitement of immigrants. Jack Najor was the only original board member to run for the first board of directors in 1982, shortly after the newly built Southfield Manor opened for business. Yelda Saroki, another original member, is a quiet and very reserved man. Zia Jalaba was an active member who at the sunset of his life dedicated himself as a deacon, serving at Mother of God Church every Sunday and so spending minimal time at the club with his family. Sam Dabish was another active church and club member who in 1975 wrote a book in Arabic about his experience in the diaspora, which included good information and details about the church, the community's first priest, and the formation of the Chaldean Iraqi Association (CIA).

April 24, 1943, is the birth date of the CIA. Detroit was the place of its birth, in a moderate middle-class hall named Danish Hall, where about 100 Chaldeans gathered. A 12-member board was elected, and Zia Nalu, a well-respected and knowledgeable man, was named the CIA president.

The CIA was the motivating force behind the purchase of 10.33 acres on Berg Road in Southfield, Michigan. Soon after the construction of Mother of God Church was completed, attention was directed to assembling enough land to build a club. Four acres were acquired, but a lot more money was needed to build a home for the club. Members were anxious and eager to raise money and see their dream become reality. On August 31, 1965, the Chaldean Iraqi Association of Michigan (CIAM) was registered in Lansing as a nonprofit organization "for the purpose of offering its members and guests banquet and dining facilities."

In 1979, the board of directors, with the support of CIAM members, decided to build a 20,000-square-foot facility. Jonna Construction Company was hired to build the new club, and Michael Nalu was the architect. Mike Sitto was the engineer. The architect, engineer, and construction company all had something in common besides being immigrants living in Michigan: they were all Chaldeans. They were all members of CIAM, and thus, Southfield Manor was a true community project. But only a handful of the original elected board members from 1943 lived to see the opening of the first *diwan khana*.

Southfield Manor was chosen as the name of the building owned by CIAM. In 1981, Southfield Manor opened for business with a dining room, an activity room for members' private use, and a banquet hall open to the public.

Most club members who lived in the 1980s, 1990s, and the first decade of the new millennium lived at a time when Mike George ruled the club and made things happen. CIAM was the mother of all organizations and still is. Chaldean Iraqi Association (CIA) was the name first chosen for the first Chaldean establishment in America. It became official at the first board meeting in 1943. On August 31, 1965, the articles of incorporation were filed and the word "Michigan" was added to the original name, which then became known as the Chaldean Iraqi Association of Michigan, (CIAM). This name continued to be used for 35 years, or just until the end of the 20th century. On June 28, 2000, another amendment was filed. This time, the word "American" was added. The name became Chaldean Iraqi American Association of Michigan (CIAAM). Almost two decades later, the name change idea is tantalizing once again. With the new generation more involved, new and fresh ideas are abundant!

In 1989, CIAM acquired Shenandoah Country Club, with an abundance of options to add in the future for youth and the next generation of golfers. Shenandoah gradually became a magnet to motivate the younger generation to join the club. The number of Chaldean golfers started to increase rapidly, with the Chaldean League competing for the Chaldean Ryder Cup.

In 2002, a memorable ground-breaking ceremony took place for a proposed 90,000-square-foot facility with a variety of activities and family enjoyment. The historic celebration was larger than any wedding, and everyone enjoyed a beautiful spread of Middle Eastern food, danced the traditional *khugga*, and sang Chaldean, Arabic, and English songs—a memory that will live longer than any marriage!

Today, 15 years later, the journey of baby steps and leaps continues as the community grows multiple times larger than all past predictions and expectations of the Chaldean diaspora in America. CIAAM will be celebrating its 75th anniversary in April 2018, a praiseworthy dream that has been a long time coming! The many past and present success stories have inspired and motivated many generations to come to America and live the American dream, all of which is illustrated herein.

One

THE CHALDEANS
IRAQ'S ORIGINAL INHABITANTS

Chaldeans are Catholics who immigrated from Mesopotamia (now Iraq), the eastern part of the Fertile Crescent, covering the land between the Tigris and Euphrates Rivers.

Chaldeans and the land of Chaldea are referenced in the Bible through the Ur of Chaldeans, which is regarded as the traditional birthplace of Abraham, the father of three major religions: Judaism, Christianity, and Islam.

The Chaldeans' mother tongue is Aramaic, which was the language spoken by Jesus Christ and is referred to as the "Jesus Language."

Christianity spread to Mesopotamia and areas of the Persian Empire as early as the first Christian century. According to ancient tradition, the apostle Thomas was the first to evangelize those regions on his journey to India. Many Chaldeans and Assyrians accepted the gospel and gradually established the Church of the East.

Before the Islamic conquest of Mesopotamia (634 AD), the majority of the population was Christian and spoke Aramaic. When the Arab Abbasids built Baghdad at the end of the eighth century as the capital of their empire, they turned to the Christian scholars of the country to spread knowledge in the fields of philosophy, medicine, chemistry, and mathematics.

Under Ottoman rule and up to the formation of the modern state of Iraq in 1921, the Christians of Mesopotamia endured several onslaughts by both the Kurds and the Turkish government. During World War I, the Christians suffered from Kurdish and Turkish persecution, which led to a wave of emigration and brought to an end many centuries of Christian presence in such cities as Adana, Urfa, Diyarbakir, Mardin, and Tur Abdin.

Chaldeans began immigrating to the United States in the early 1900s. The rapidly growing auto industry attracted the largest share to Detroit. One factor that made Michigan desirable was the presence of the Lebanese, who had immigrated from greater Syria and established churches that served Mass similar to the Chaldean Rite. Another factor was the proximity to Canada, where other Chaldeans had immigrated just a few years earlier.

JESUS LANGUAGE. Aramaic, the mother tongue of all Chaldeans, was the native language of Mesopotamia, where Christianity was the religion of the majority until the Islamic conquest of 634 AD. Aramaic is clearly distinct from the spoken language used in northern Iraqi Christian villages. Educated Chaldeans who know both languages call the church language Chaldean and the spoken language Sureth. Most Chaldeans do not understand the church language, only the dialect they use every day. The majority of Chaldeans speak Arabic fluently, because it is the official language of Iraq. Today, Aramaic is considered an endangered language, and Chaldean community leaders have launched efforts to keep it alive. (Author's collection.)

ON A MISSION. Missionaries with medical and teaching skills were welcomed in Iraq, but they won few converts. The Arab Muslim majority wanted knowledge, not Christian ethics. French, British, and American missionaries and educators of the late 19th and early 20th centuries brought their religion to the Arab world and established a few churches and schools, including the Dominican School for Boys in Mosul, which was open to both Muslims and Christians. Iraq had its share of Presbyterians and Anglicans, and some converted, but most Muslims steered clear. The missionary presence was questioned by some in the Iraqi Muslim majority; some missionaries described their teachings as "awakening" and were thought to encourage revolutionary sparks among the Iraqi youth. (Courtesy of Catholic University of America.)

THINK FORD FIRST. Among the many reasons for coming to Detroit, Henry Ford's revolutionary decision in 1914 to pay workers $5 a day—more than double the typical wage—was by far the biggest factor for Chaldeans. As news spread of the unprecedented wage, about 25 Chaldean families moved from Fort Williams, Canada, and settled in Detroit's Eastside, in the vicinity of Jefferson Avenue and East Grand Boulevard, reaching north to the Highland Park border. Workers were required to learn English, and the Ford English School had more than 2,200 students by 1916. (Author's collection.)

HAPPY 12TH ANNIVERSARY, FATHER BIDAWID. The small but rapidly growing community celebrates the 12th anniversary of newly arrived priest Thomas Bidawid, seen sitting at the head table on May 15, 1947. Chaldean Rite Catholics in Detroit were without the services of a priest of their own for more than 30 years. They attended Mass and held special events like weddings and funerals at St. Maron's Church at 1555 East Congress Street in Detroit. St. Maron's Lebanese Christians had similar rituals and also spoke Aramaic before adopting Arabic over three centuries ago. Father Bidawid named the first Chaldean church "Mother of God," a most interesting title in light of the rite's former Nestorian connection. The name also served as a symbol of its unity with Rome. (Courtesy of Margie Gabbara Atto, Chaldean Cultural Center.)

SIMPLE LIFE. Many of the first settlers were illiterate in both English and Arabic, since Aramaic was the dominant language of the villages of northern Iraq. Village life was very simple—there was no running water, no electricity, no gas, no cars, and no phones, but there were donkeys, mules, and horses for the wealthy. Most of the Chaldean immigrants who arrived in the United States prior to the 1940s came by boat, and to this day, those who lack English skills or fall short on picking up American customs are pejoratively called "boaters." The Okka Jarbou family is pictured in Telkaif in 1939. Standing from left to right are Okka, the head of the household; Khoki, his wife; Jammo, their daughter in law; and Shabib; her husband and Okka and Khoki's son. Seated are Nissan (left) and Goggi, Okka and Khoki's other sons. (Courtesy of Nadine Dickow Rabban.)

CHURCH FIRST. The church was the center of life in Telkaif, a tradition that was carried all the way to Detroit and is maintained to this day. In this photograph, mothers and daughters are in the courtyard of Sacred Heart Church in Telkaif, known to historians as the grounds where Zenophon, the commander of a Greek army, passed through town while chasing Darius, the Persian king, in 401 BC. Women worked tirelessly around the church, cleaning and teaching children to pray and read the Bible. (Courtesy of Chaldean Catholic Diocese.)

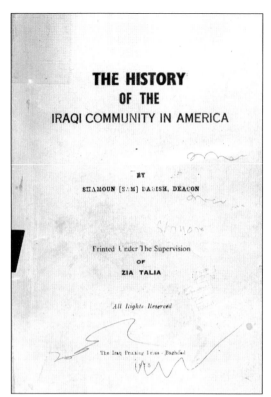

THE HISTORY
OF THE
IRAQI COMMUNITY IN AMERICA

BY

SHAMOUN [SAM] DABISH, DEACON

Printed Under The Supervision
OF
ZIA TALIA

The Iraq Printing Press - Baghdad
1975

CHALDEAN DIASPORA. Shamoun (Sam) Dabish was the first Chaldean immigrant to write a book about the Chaldean diaspora community. *The History of the Iraqi Community in America* was written in Arabic and published in 1975 by the Iraqi Printing Press in Baghdad. His book offered a brief summary of the early Chaldeans in Detroit, covering the hard work and tireless efforts necessary to establish the first Chaldean church in Detroit and the first ever Chaldean organization in America, the Chaldean Iraqi Association. His dedication and involvement in the church as deacon, parish council member, elected CIA member, and author prove his faith, affection, and love for his community. (Both, author's collection.)

Traditional Family in Telkaif. It was very common for married sons to live with their father and mother under the same roof, each with their own family. Each married son would occupy a room or two within the same house. The married brothers worked together with their other siblings on the farm or at their shop selling household items. Daughters helped their mothers with the cooking and cleaning. (Courtesy of Salim Kas Shamoun.)

Village Life. Life in an Iraqi village can make a visitor feel like an alien from another planet, and both the young and old are eager to check out a stranger, which can make a guest uncomfortable. These children filling a narrow alley of Telkaif in 1986 are today's immigrants who have found great success. The kids in this photograph, many years later and without exception, found a new home in Southeast Michigan and prospered in many businesses, such as convenience stores, gas stations, restaurants, cell phone businesses, and the hospitality industry. (Author's collection.)

17

Moving Up. Chaldeans left their villages in search of a better life and higher standard of living. Larger cities like Baghdad, Mosul, and Basra were the target for young and ambitious Chaldeans. Baghdad, being the most vibrant, attracted the most. To this day, families relocate from Telkaif to settle in the capital city, which has more than 7.6 million residents. This photograph was taken in Baghdad in the summer of 1958. (Courtesy of Eddie Bacall.)

A Time of Unrest. Iraq, more than any other Arab country, took the lead in a number of revolutions, toppling governments and engaging in wars with surrounding countries. Executions of Iraqi citizens were a common scene in the streets in Baghdad in the late 1950s, 1960s, and 1970s. Pictured here in the early 1960s is a group of young Chaldeans who are leaving the country to study abroad. For most, the trip abroad was a one-way ticket. (Courtesy of Eddie Bacall.)

ALL TOGETHER NOW. Chaldeans have large, close families and are always ready to welcome newcomers, especially those who have never traveled abroad before or do not speak English as they adjust to life in America. Large gatherings are just a typical Sunday in many Chaldean households. Those who have come before consider it a duty to help their cousins—official and otherwise—as they assimilate. (Courtesy of Julia Najor Hallahan.)

LAUNCHING POINT. The earliest immigrants were introduced to the grocery business by Syrians and Lebanese from Greater Syria. The trade required little training or English language skills and was a lucrative way for newcomers to make a living. A considerable number of Chaldean households remain in the retail grocery business today but have also branched out into many other industries, including real estate, hotels, and telecommunications. Many young people are entering the medical and legal professions. (Courtesy of Chaldean Cultural Center.)

STRIVING FORWARD. Community members, many of them new immigrants, pose with Fr. Thomas Bidawid (fifth from left) in 1947. Many trials faced these newcomers, including the need to learn a new language, find work, and secure a place to live. Despite the challenges, they were motivated to seek a life away from war, famine, and religious and political persecution. Was the price of freedom worth the sacrifice? The answer is unfailingly yes, and most Chaldeans have thrived in their new land. (Courtesy of Mary Ann Jalaba Yono.)

THE CHANCE OF A LIFETIME. There was a backlash of intimidation and assassinations during the 1950s, 1960s, and early 1970s, and the Christian community was targeted indiscriminately. This was followed by a wave of migration of Christians from Mosul to Baghdad; at a later time, many found themselves fortunate to come to the United States. Pictured here is the reunited Kouza family in the early 1970s; from left to right are Majid (Mike), brother Lyon, Mariam (their mother), Adel (Eddie), Zuhair (Steve), and Wejdi (Jack). (Courtesy of Linda Kouza Jeberaeel.)

HOME AWAY FROM HOME. During the 1970s and 1980s, Detroit's Seven Mile Road area between Woodward Avenue and John R Street was as Brooklyn and Queens were to immigrants in New York, offering reasonably priced housing, a short drive to work, and a convenient church nearby. The Middle Eastern stores of Seven Mile, including a coffee shop, bakery, restaurant, and market, were not unlike the Bab Al-Toub business district in central Mosul. Today, Seven Mile has fallen on hard times and has yet to experience the renaissance that has revitalized Detroit's downtown area. (Author's collection.)

CHAI TIME. Tea shops (*chai-khana*) like this were the social center for all newcomers; men with bushy dark mustaches would come to see their newly arrived friends and relatives and catch up on current events in the smoke-filled rooms. They played cards, dominos, and backgammon as they drank chai or Turkish coffee and ate *tikka* (chunks of beef or lamb with onions and tomatoes on a skewer). Politics and business were lively topics of debate. (Author's collection.)

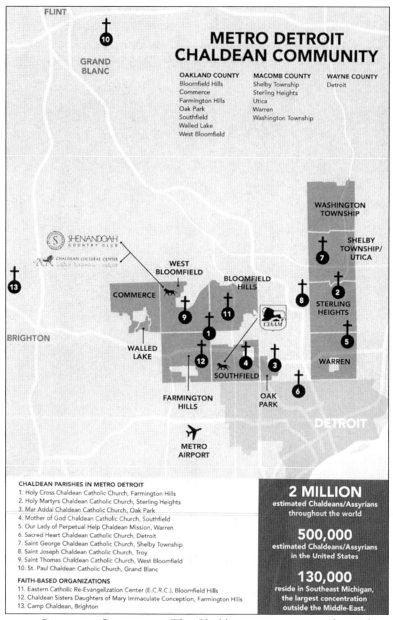

METRO DETROIT CHALDEAN COMMUNITY

FLINT

GRAND BLANC

OAKLAND COUNTY	MACOMB COUNTY	WAYNE COUNTY
Bloomfield Hills	Shelby Township	Detroit
Commerce	Sterling Heights	
Farmington Hills	Utica	
Oak Park	Warren	
Southfield	Washington Township	
Walled Lake		
West Bloomfield		

WASHINGTON TOWNSHIP

SHELBY TOWNSHIP/ UTICA

SHENANDOAH COUNTRY CLUB

CHALDEAN CULTURAL CENTER

WEST BLOOMFIELD

BLOOMFIELD HILLS

STERLING HEIGHTS

COMMERCE

BRIGHTON

WALLED LAKE

WARREN

SOUTHFIELD

FARMINGTON HILLS

OAK PARK

DETROIT

METRO AIRPORT

CHALDEAN PARISHES IN METRO DETROIT
1. Holy Cross Chaldean Catholic Church, Farmington Hills
2. Holy Martyrs Chaldean Catholic Church, Sterling Heights
3. Mar Addai Chaldean Catholic Church, Oak Park
4. Mother of God Chaldean Catholic Church, Southfield
5. Our Lady of Perpetual Help Chaldean Mission, Warren
6. Sacred Heart Chaldean Catholic Church, Detroit
7. Saint George Chaldean Catholic Church, Shelby Township
8. Saint Joseph Chaldean Catholic Church, Troy
9. Saint Thomas Chaldean Catholic Church, West Bloomfield
10. St. Paul Chaldean Catholic Church, Grand Blanc

FAITH-BASED ORGANIZATIONS
11. Eastern Catholic Re-Evangelization Center (E.C.R.C.), Bloomfield Hills
12. Chaldean Sisters Daughters of Mary Immaculate Conception, Farmington Hills
13. Camp Chaldean, Brighton

2 MILLION
estimated Chaldeans/Assyrians throughout the world

500,000
estimated Chaldeans/Assyrians in the United States

130,000
reside in Southeast Michigan, the largest concentration outside the Middle-East.

METRO DETROIT CHALDEAN COMMUNITY. The Chaldean community made good use of the job opportunities in metro Detroit thanks to its proximity to Canada and the booming auto industry. Relatives, cousins, and friends followed in the footsteps of their predecessors, and before they knew it, a community grew up around the concentration of Chaldeans in three counties: Oakland, Macomb, and Wayne. From the 1920s to the 1950s, the majority of the Chaldean community was concentrated in Detroit. In the 1960s and 1970s, Chaldeans moved to Southfield, Oak Park, and other surrounding cities. During the 1980s and 1990s, Chaldeans expanded to Farmington, West Bloomfield, Warren, and Sterling Heights. In the 2000s, Chaldeans continued to spread out into other cities like Bloomfield Hills, Troy, and Shelby Township. Chaldeans lived in the areas that surrounded their churches and their beloved club, whether Southfield Manor or Shenandoah Country Club, and continue to live in these areas today. (Art by Alex Lumelsky.)

Two

Diwan Khana

A Community Club is Born

As the numbers of new immigrants continued to grow, their roots in Detroit deepened, and they successfully grew their businesses, primarily supermarkets and grocery stores. Their hard work and dedication earned them a comfortable living and the confidence to be more productive and useful to their community and people.

In the 1930s, active leaders of the small community, which numbered about 45 to 50 families, decided to establish an organization to address the community's needs. Building a church and bringing in a Chaldean Rite priest who could speak and preach in Aramaic was a major goal, as was aiding the poor back home in Iraq and helping emigrants buy their passage aboard a ship to the United States.

The venue to gather and discuss ideas, socialize, resolve disputes, plan, and organize was commonly referred to as diwan khana, loosely translated as "gathering place."

The first announced meeting was held in the fall of 1937 by a group of Chaldeans who lived and worked in Detroit at Rouge Park. The attendees agreed to name the new organization the Chaldean Iraqi Association, or CIA. Not much happened to move the idea forward until the summer of 1941, when another meeting was held, and there was another meeting the next year.

Finally, a general membership meeting was scheduled for 9:30 p.m. on April 24, 1943, at the Danish Hall, located at 1775 Forest Avenue in Detroit. (The late start was so people had time to close their stores.) In true Chaldean fashion, the meeting did not actually start until 10:00 p.m. after everyone had the chance to mix and mingle.

All registered members paid $25 as an introductory fee and agreed to dues of $5 a month or $60 a year. That night, nominations were made for the inaugural board of directors. With less than an hour to go before midnight, the birth of one of the oldest and most rooted establishments was announced. The 12-member board was elected, and Zia Nalu was chosen as its first president.

I AM A PROUD MEMBER. Anyone of Chaldean descent was entitled to enjoy everything the club had to offer, but had to comply with the membership eligibility requirements, such as being 21 years of age, proven to be of good character, recommended by two active members, and the approval of two thirds of the board of trustees present. It has been debated whether it is legal to not accept anyone not of Chaldean descent, which means a non-Chaldean cannot join the club! "I believe that CIAAM is able to discriminate in its membership selection without violating any laws, based on the theory that we have the freedom of association first amendment right," said legal counsel and longtime CIAAM member Burt S. Kassab. (Both, courtesy of CIAAM files and records.)

LIFE IN A NEW LAND. After Mass, everyone gathered for social time in the basement of Mother of God Church, located at Hamilton Avenue and Euclid Street in Detroit. This picture, taken shortly after the church opened to the community in 1948, includes many Chaldean women who were enjoying the American ideals of individual freedom and equality. (Courtesy of Tobia Hakim archives.)

GOODWILL AMBASSADORS. Chaldeans in Detroit maintained a good relationship with the government in Baghdad. CIAAM members took it upon themselves to act as ambassadors to Iraq. Iraq's ambassador to the United States, Dr. Nasser al-Hani, is seen here (center, with sunglasses) in August 1961 being greeted at the Beirut airport in Lebanon by a group of Chaldeans from Detroit, including Salim Sarafa, Jack Najor, and Yelda Saroki. They were accompanied by other family and friends, including members of the Murad Al-Sheikh family, one of the most influential Chaldean families in Baghdad. (Courtesy of Paul Murad.)

LOVE AND MARRIAGE. Large and lavish wedding receptions are a community tradition, so when the new club was built, special attention was paid to that side of the business. Wedding parties were a profit center for the club, and not just Chaldean weddings—by the mid-1980s, parties from outside the community made up more than a third of the banquet business. Banquet revenue, first at Southfield Manor and then its replacement, Shenandoah Country Club, was the backbone of CIAM since its inception. In America, wedding ceremonies are held in church, rather than at the bride's home, as was the village custom. Chaldeans are Eastern Rite Catholics who are united with the Roman Catholic Church but have their own distinctive style of church structure, penitential customs, and pattern of prayers during Mass. (Above, courtesy of Tammy Shouneyia Shammas; below, courtesy of Junior Jwad.)

First Elected
BOARD OF DIRECTORS - APRIL 24, 1943
Chaldean Iraqi Association "C.I.A"

Zia Nalu
President

Peter Zoma
Vice President

Yalda "Joe" Saroki
Treasurer

Joe Najor
Secretary

Shamoun "Sam"
Dabish

Zia Jalaba

Birth of C.I.A
General Membership Meeting
Date of Meeting: April 24, 1943
Time of Meeting: 9:30pm
Place of Meeting: Danish Hall
1775 West Forest, Detroit, MI 48208
(NO Chaldean time PLEASE)

Jack Najor

alab Neiman
Luccia

Joe Acho

George Najor

Dawood Koury

Dawood Kilano

BIRTH OF CIA. All of these foreign-born citizens had in common a love for their community and a burning desire to do good works, to build a church, and to establish a facility large enough to accommodate everyone at weddings, baptisms, and other special events. Multiple meetings and gatherings took place during the late 1930s and early 1940s, with heated discussions among the new Chaldean immigrants. But none of these meetings bore fruit or resulted in the formation of CIA. It took a giant step by a few diehard Chaldeans to get the tiny community to agree to meet on April 24, 1943, to formally establish the Chaldean Iraqi Association and elect a board of directors that was hard-working, had morals and ethics, and was willing to serve. (Art by Cesar Yaldo of Exclusive Imagery.)

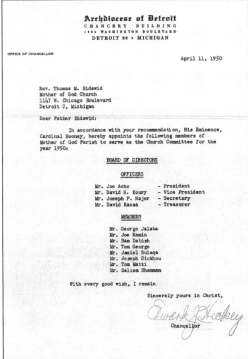

CREATING A COMMUNITY CHURCH. In the 1930s, leaders of the Chaldean community, which by that time numbered approximately 120, began to plan for the establishment of a parish of their own rite. A group of Chaldean men including Joe Acho, Sam Dabish, David Kassa (Kassab), Dawood Koury, Jack Najor, and Zia Nalu met with the archbishop of Detroit, Cardinal Edward Mooney, in 1945. Cardinal Mooney was instrumental in the establishment of a Chaldean Rite parish in Detroit. Through his influence, Chaldean patriarch Joseph Emmanuel Thomas II, from his seat in Mosul, Iraq, sent Rev. Thomas Bidawid to be the first Chaldean pastor in Detroit in February 1947. On August 15, 1948, Father Bidawid named the new church Mother of God, a symbol of the church's unity with Rome. That was significant because the Chaldean Rite was formerly tied to the Nestorians, who rejected the Virgin Mary's right to that title. On April 11, 1950, Cardinal Mooney signed the letter of approval of church plans at left. (Both, courtesy of Barbara Jalaba Gorge.)

ESSENTIAL READING. For nearly half a century, the Chaldean telephone directory, which was published through the Mother of God Parish, served as the main source of census data on the community, which was still relatively small. The directory listed the name, address, telephone number, and often the family size and the occupation of the head of the household. These days, computer technology has put an end to its existence. (Author's collection.)

GOTTA DANCE. No celebration or gathering is complete without friends and relatives, young and old, joining hands to form a line and shake, shake, shake. What one does not see is the fire behind the traditional dances. While the music may be what gets people on the dance floor, it is the cultural heritage that links them to village life and cherished traditions and keeps their feet moving. (Courtesy of Raad Kathawa.)

A Festive Time. The annual Arab and Chaldean Festival in downtown Detroit featured Middle Eastern food, clothing, jewelry, music, and traditional Arabic and Northern Iraqi Christian dance. CIAM members of all ages were eager to donate some of their free time to work at the events, which raised thousands of dollars for good causes, paid off the newly purchased land's delinquent property taxes, and helped launch a membership drive. Among the volunteers were Dave Nona, Salah Zoma, Sabah Hermiz Summa, the Talia brothers, Malika and Josephine Sesi, Yvonne Nona, Najib Karmo, and Ilham Shayota. (Courtesy of Sabah Hermiz Summa.)

Young and Ambitious. Young Chaldeans had a lot in common—language, religion, village of origin, and often bloodlines—and were eager to preserve their heritage and traditions in the face of growing Arab nationalism. They were torn between their ethnic identity and their national origin. (Courtesy of Ismat Karmo.)

CHALDEANS ON THE MAP. The Christians of Iraq were concentrated in villages throughout northern Iraq, and those from rural areas spoke no language other than Syriac. Other Christians in larger cities spoke Arabic, the official language of the country, and they lost their Syriac at some stage of their city life. In the villages, it was customary for families to sleep in the open air on the terraces on the roofs of their houses. (Both, courtesy of Saher Yaldo of Exclusive Imagery.)

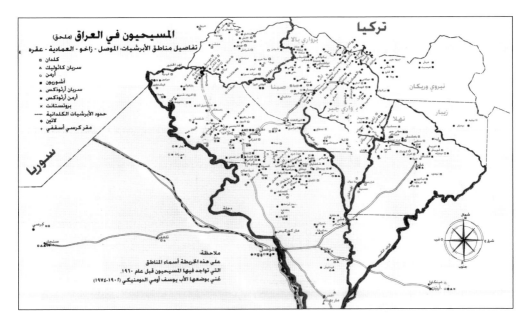

DANISH HALL. Once upon a time, this was the official clubhouse of the Chaldeans, "having a baptism one day and a wedding the next day," according to Salim Kas Shamoun. He was born in Iraq in 1924 and got married at Danish Hall in Detroit in the 1950s. With tears in his eyes, Shamoun remembers how beautiful the hall was, and the neighborhood. Danish Hall was built in 1915 for Scandinavian Americans. The Chaldeans used the hall for their meetings, events, and weddings. By the mid-1970s, ownership of the hall changed hands, and it was closed in 2001. The 100-year-old social hall is going through a renovation and a name change as Danish Brotherhood Hall. (Courtesy of Danish Brotherhood Hall.)

CIVIL UNREST. The July 1967 riot in Detroit provided an opportunity for Chaldean merchants to fill the needs of a city abandoned by the big supermarket chains like A&P, Great Scott, and Farmer Jack. Today, Chaldeans control 80 percent of the grocery businesses in Detroit, selling food and household items. (Courtesy of the *Detroit Free Press.*)

DE - WAN - KHANA
Friday, April 26, 2002

Appetizers

- Hummous, Tabouleh and Baba Ganough
- Vegetables and dip
- Sesame bread with a pesto sauce with roasted garlic
- Labne and Zetoune

Salad

Baba's house salad – mixed greens, cherry tomatoes, parmesan cheese and Jacob's homemade dressing

Dinner

- Traditional Dolma
- Gerger with lamb
- Mazgouff
- Salmon with sauce
- Beef Shish Kabob

Dessert

- Emakacha
- Baklawa
- Fresh Cut Fruit
- Simsimia – fresh from Mosul
- Homemade Kuleche

BABA KHOSHABA
"Telkeppe Kitchen"

FINE FEAST. Diwan khana, a special room or guesthouse where males would gather, was on the mind of many early immigrants. The idea behind the term has been modified over the years, as have some customs like taking one's wife out, accompanying a female friend, and serving a variety of food and alcohol, none of which were the norm of the traditional diwan khana. Chaldeans took the idea and modified it to their new cultural reality by including both men and women and elaborate meals with a great variety of food. Since the roots of diwan khana were stuck in the minds of the seniors of the club, they decided to call their special evening gathering "De-Wan-Khana," where they enjoyed discussions about world affairs, the grocery business, club management, and elections. Some would sip a beer, but most consumed black tea with cardamom and cinnamon or Turkish coffee in its original form—black and strong. The group included Bishop Ibrahim Ibrahim, Lou Kenaya, Karim Dabish, Aziz Najor, Jamil Yono, Salman Sesi, Salim Sarafa, Karim Sarafa, Mansour Sitto, Joseph Nadhir, and Gabe Sheena. (Author's collection.)

Chaldean Iraqi American Association of Michigan

C.I.A.A.M

Directory

CIAAM SHENANDOAH Country Club

New Shenandoah Country Club

BY THE BOOK. The first CIAAM directory was published in June 2002. It was one of the promises made by the author of this book in his two-minute speech when running for the board of CIAAM for the 2001–2002 two-year term. With the support of the board of directors and the tireless efforts of Zuhair Antone, the first directory included a brief history of CIAAM, the current and former board of directors, maps, and the layouts of Southfield Manor and Shenandoah, both of which were owned and operated by the members of CIAAM. The book also included a membership directory, the club constitution and bylaws, and club policies. The staff and committee responsibilities and guidelines were published in both English and Arabic, but not Aramaic. (Author's collection.)

Three

SOUTHFIELD MANOR
CIAM's First Home

In 1965, after a membership meeting, a final draft of the constitution and bylaws were approved and the articles of incorporation were filed with the State of Michigan by the club's president, Salim Sarafa. It was decided by the majority of voting members to be a nonprofit organization known as the Chaldean Iraqi Association of Michigan (CIAM).

The organization started with 60 members, and within the first two years, membership doubled. The board of directors, with the support and help of Fr. George Garmo from Mother of God Church, purchased a three-acre site from the Archdiocese of Detroit on November 28, 1968, for $19,500. About an acre had been purchased from Norman and Jennie Bennett on April 29, 1967, for $16,500. CIAM now owned four acres of contiguous land.

In late 1977, diligent efforts were begun to build a new club. CIAM had accumulated a total of around $600,000 in the bank, and the four acres were owned free and clear of any debt. It was time to move forward with the Chaldean dream of building a social club and community center.

Michael Nalu was the architect hired to design the facility. He was later joined by another Chaldean architect, Michael Sitto, who worked closely with Jonna Construction Company. After a few months, the plan was ready for the final blessing of the CIAM board. But Michael George, the visionary leader and president at the time, expressed concern that the facility was too small and that the kitchen would not function as needed. While everyone on the board liked his ideas, they all said in one voice, "But we do not have the money to build a club this size!" Michael George's answer was very simple: "Don't worry, I will take care of that."

Sure enough, new plans were soon underway, and a loan of $2 million was approved by Community National Bank of Pontiac, with the condition of a personal guaranty of two diehard club members and advocates, Michael George and past president Manuel Meram.

A contract was signed with Jonna Construction Company in the spring of 1979 for the total amount of $895,000 plus any construction change orders, furniture, fixtures, and equipment, and any out-of-pocket expenses.

Southfield Manor. ～ Southfield, Michigan

Betty Trombetta

LAND IN HAND. Fr. George Garmo, pastor of Mother of God Church on Hamilton Street and Glynn Court in Detroit, finalized the purchase of 10.3 acres on Berg Road in Southfield for $50,000 in June 1964. In 1968, a four-acre lot was assembled consisting of three acres acquired from Mother of God and an additional acre purchased in 1967 from private owners who lived in Ohio, Norman and Jennie Bennett. Father Garmo spearheaded the efforts to carve a piece of land to build the long-awaited clubhouse and Chaldean cultural center. His plan to sell those three acres to CIAM to build Southfield Manor was initially rejected by the Catholic archbishop of Detroit. It took increased pressure from influential community leaders and the strong support of Father Garmo to finalize the sale under the condition that the property would return to the seller if CIAM decided not to build the proposed club. (Above, art by Betty Trombetta; below, courtesy of CIAAM files and records.)

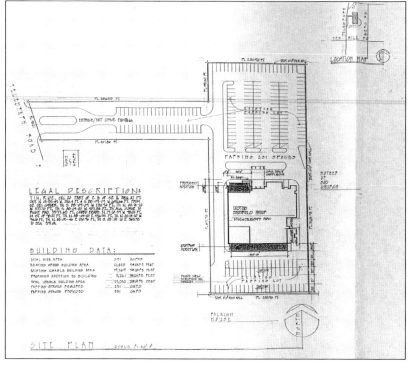

MISSION TO ACCOMPLISH. In 1980, as construction of the new club was underway, a financial crisis surfaced due to construction overruns resulting in many change orders. The need to raise more money was on everybody's mind. The availability of an Iraqi government grant was circulated, and the temptation had some club members drooling. But the mood was somewhat sour and skeptical, and opinions were divided on what to do. Who was right? Who was wrong? No one knew. Was the Iraqi government seeking influence? Absolutely. An opposing group including the Mansour brothers (Peter and Drs. Noori and Jacob), Ralph Ayar, Cal Abbo, Louis Stephen, and Adnan Gabbara made the rounds, knocking on the door of every Chaldean store owner to raise money to resume construction. They succeeded in collecting a considerable amount of cash, but the total did not tilt the scale away from the government grant. On June 5, 1980, the final deciding vote by CIAM members was 69-59 in favor of receiving the grant, and the Iraqi government's $150,000 was accepted. (Above, courtesy of *The Michigan Catholic*; below, courtesy of Dr. Talat Karmo.)

the American goal... **THE MOON!**

the Chaldean goal...

THE CLUBHOUSE **?**

CLUB DREAMS. In 1970, the year after Neil Armstrong turned a dream into reality by walking on the moon, this illustration was circulated to the members of CIAM of another dream about to come true. But to this day, no one knows who came up with the name "Southfield Manor" or why. (Courtesy of Amir Denha.)

GROUP EFFORT. Many were involved in the Chaldean Iraqi Association of Michigan's construction of Southfield Manor. Michael Nalu was the architect and Jonna Construction Company the contractor. Community National Bank financed the project with a $2 million loan. Construction began in 1979, and Southfield Manor officially opened on May 31, 1981, at 25626 Telegraph Road in Southfield with the telephone number 248-352-9020. (Courtesy of Dr. John Kassid.)

NEW CLUB, NEW BOARD. In October 1981, the general membership voted for a new board of directors, and the election committee, chaired by accountant Georgis Garmo, announced the 10 winners. The seven candidates with the highest vote totals would serve for two years, and the following three members would form the "reserve board." Pictured here is the board of directors from 1981 to 1983. From left to right are (seated) Joseph Nadhir, Bernie Garmo, and George P. Najor; (standing) Najib Karmo, Salim Sarafa, Manuel Meram, Michael J. George, Badie Bodiya, Ralph Ayar, and Cal Abbo. (Courtesy of Ralph Ayar.)

A CHANGE IN STATUS. After Southfield Manor operated as a nonprofit social club for more than a year, its status was amended to become a for-profit corporation. The change was made official on June 21, 1982. (Courtesy of CIAAM files and records.)

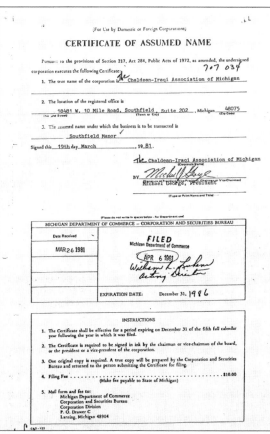

WHAT'S IN A NAME? Southfield Manor became the official name of the clubhouse on April 6, 1981. The applicant was Chaldean Iraqi Association of Michigan. The registered office was 18481 West 10 Mile Road in Southfield, because the long-awaited club was near completion but not yet open. (Courtesy of CIAAM files and records.)

WHO DOESN'T REMEMBER THIS? This familiar sign was visible when approaching the steep hill to the club entrance just off Telegraph Road. That was the only entrance to the club until an access was opened between the church and the club in case of fire or emergency. Tens of thousands of people still remember this sign that stood for a quarter of a century. In July 1979, the Michigan Department of Transportation granted Jonna Construction Company the right to utilize the existing 40-foot curb as the main entrance to the club. The sign now hangs on the lower level of Shenandoah Country Club. (Author's collection.)

THE PLACE TO BE. Southfield Manor totaled 26,431 square feet and had 231 parking spaces. It was known as one of the premier banquet facilities in metro Detroit, with a capacity of up to 600 guests in the main banquet hall, approximately 100 people in the West Room, and 118 people in the private restaurant. For more than 20 years, Southfield Manor was the place to have a party with fabulous food. A major renovation in 1996 at a cost of nearly $2 million expanded the kitchen, added a meeting room and game rooms, put on a new roof, and upgraded the HVAC systems. Located next to the pool room, the restaurant and bar served hundreds of thousands of dinners and millions of drinks. Southfield Manor, in the heart of the CIAM community, provided memories for generations of Chaldean families and guests. Being next door to Mother of God Church gave the club, known for its friendly access, carefree environment, and cozy family atmosphere, additional value and prestige. (Both, author's collection.)

THE LION'S BAR. Some of the club members became regulars and familiar faces to the operating staff. Salim Sarafa was known for his Courvoisier cognac and Lucky Strike cigarettes, Charlie Asker for his Jack Daniels, and Thomas Denha for his Napa Valley red wine. The majority of silver-haired seniors and some of the jet-black-haired (pretending to be) juniors split their choices between scotch and cognac, depending on the day. A popular sight was the Zeer brothers—Farook, Eddie, and Kays—who enjoyed life at day's end. They always occupied the south side of the well-stocked bar and liked everything in it, not discriminating between scotch or cognac. Other members of the younger generation preferred wine or beer, while the newly arrived Iraqi natives would request *arak*, a popular drink from back home known as the "milk of the lions" for its strength and long-lasting impact. Above is a bartender getting ready to open, and below is Fadi Abdelnour, the last general manager of Southfield Manor, in the members' dining room in 2001. (Both, author's collection.)

COMMUNION AT SHENANDOAH. Southfield Manor continued to serve the community until the purchase of Shenandoah Country Club in 1989, which then became the site of numerous social, political, and religious functions, such as weddings, engagements, funerals, and communion parties. Pictured here is Caroline Mary Bacall's first holy communion in the spring of 1993 at the original Shenandoah banquet center. (Author's collection.)

HAPPY 50TH BIRTHDAY, EDDIE. On July 14, 2003, a surprise party was planned by the family and friends of Eddie Bacall. With drinks in hand and smiling faces, everyone had a great time. Eddie has not yet recovered from the shock of a celebration he did not expect. (Author's collection.)

43

LEGAL TENDER. A stock certificate, also known as a share certificate, is a legal document of ownership. It has no face value but discloses the name of the association as registered in the state of Michigan at the time of issuance. It also reveals the member's name and membership number. Every club member in good standing holds one share. Just like legal currency notes in the United States, every share certificate comes with the signature of the treasurer and the association president. (Courtesy of Sohail Dayimiya.)

EASTER BRUNCH AT THE MANOR. Southfield Manor was the place to be for brunch on Easter or Mother's Day. It was also the site of many family reunions where the entire clan would show up for traditional lunch or dinner and the newer generation got to know their first, second, and third cousins. Southfield Manor remains a cherished legacy to all who enjoyed the many special gatherings the club had to offer. Seen here is the Bacall family in the overflow room after Easter brunch in 1991. (Author's collection.)

HE IS THE MAN OF MY SALT. Southfield Manor became known as the "Chaldean Club," gradually earning its reputation and popularity for authentic Middle Eastern dishes and ancient Mesopotamian recipes. Chaldeans of Mesopotamia regarded salt with significant meaning, such as loyalty and faithfulness. If a Mesopotamian said, "he is the man of my salt," it meant, "he is my friend." The symbolic linkage of salt and bread was established thousands of years ago. To this day, natives of Iraq share *zaad wa maleh* (food/bread and salt) as a reference to a close brotherly bond. Pictured here is the private members' dining room, which served hundreds of thousands of dinners from 1981 to 2006 before Southfield Manor was sold. (Both, author's collection.)

GROWING PAINS. In the late 1980s, the board of directors was overwhelmed by the pressure of the club's day-to-day operations and its absentee owner style of operation. After much discussion, it was agreed at a general membership meeting to hire a management company to run the banquet hall and member restaurant. The board believed this would cut costs and increase profitability to meet mortgage debt and build a reserve for future remodeling and renovation. Oak Management was given the contract to do just that. It went well for a while, but in the end, members complained of poor service and lower-quality food. Oak Management was dismissed, and the club went back to square one. After another unsuccessful experience with a second management company, HDS, the decision was made to tweak the in-house operation of the club. (Above, courtesy of Raad Kathawa; below, author's collection.)

Four

CIAAM

Club Committees and Activities

To build an organization of any kind, the grassroots elements of people and staff are needed to plan and execute goals and objectives. Club committees are typically small groups of members who act as the bees who gather the nectar to produce honey to benefit the greater hive of the club and the Chaldean community at large. Additionally, their work for the club reflects the character of the members.

Various committees include executive (the board of directors), education, legal and bylaws, elections, social and public relations, and several other semi-permanent committees such as planning, awards, membership drives, and finance that are activated as needed. The basic intent of these committees is to continually upgrade the knowledge level of the members and their families so they can take an active role in shaping the future of their community for many generations to come, just as the Chaldean pioneers did many decades ago.

One of the most important committees is the board of directors, which consists of nine members elected as representatives of the membership. Their duties are at all times conducted in the best interest of the membership as a whole, including but not limited to overseeing all club services, establishing administrative policies, setting priorities based on planning, and working with the committees to improve the quality of the services.

The board of directors may authorize to appoint a special and standing committee among the members of the club as it deems necessary. The board defines the functions and duties of these committees. Meetings of the committees are governed by the same rules as specified for the board of directors.

Preserving the nearly 75-year-old establishment has not been easy. Future generations of Chaldeans have the responsibility of carrying the torch and being faithful guardians of their heritage.

CONSTITUTION
and
BY-LAWS
Chaldean-Iraqi Association
of Michigan
(C.I.A.M.)
Amended June, 1977

ARTICLE I — NAME:
The name of this non-profit corporation is the Chaldean-Iraqi Association of Michigan, known as CIAM.

ARTICLE II — PURPOSES:
Its general purposes shall be the following:

a. To acquire and/or build a center for its members.

b. To further the social and cultural affairs of its members.

c. To assist financially students of special talents.

d. To render assistance to the members of the community whenever deemed necessary.

e. To acquire and hold real estate needed to establish a center for its members.

ARTICLE III — MEMBERSHIP ELIGIBILITY

1. Honorary Membership:

a. An honorary perpetual membership shall be granted by the Board of Trustees to an individual who contributes $5,000.00 in cash or its equivalent.

2. Regular Membership:

a. Anyone of Chaldean descent or Chaldean spouse shall be entitled to its active membership if in good standing.

b. No membership is granted to anyone unless the individual has attained his or her twenty-first birthday and has proved to be of good character.

c. Applications are processed after the recommendation of two active members and the approval of two-thirds of the Board of Trustees present.

d. Any Chaldean organization which has been active for a period of one year and the Constitution and By-Laws of which are accepted by the Association may apply for a group membership and the procedure applied should follow that of the individual membership. Membership of individual or organization (regardless of its size) shall have only one vote.

ABIDING BY THE RULES. The constitution and bylaws of CIAM serve the organization and its members as if the club was a country. The rules and regulations govern the operation of the club and ensure the comfort and enjoyment of all members, their families, and guests. The management team is authorized and empowered to implement and enforce all rules, regulations, and CIAM board decisions. (Courtesy of CIAAM files and records.)

THE GOVERNING BODY. The board of directors, also known as the board of trustees, consists of nine executive members. Elections are held annually to fill the expiring terms. Each elected board member is limited to two consecutive terms. The board then elects the positions of president, vice president, treasurer, and secretary among itself. Directors must be citizens of the United States, never convicted of a felony, and of course, people of good standing. This board agenda is from January 2002. (Author's collection.)

DOING THE MOST GOOD. The board of directors oversees the entire operation, interprets bylaws when necessary, enacts and enforces all rules and regulations, and operates the club in the best interest of the members. Shown here in the members' dining room at Southfield Manor is the CIAAM board of directors for 2002, along with the general managers of Southfield Manor and Shenandoah Country Club. (Author's collection.)

C.I.A.M. News Bulletin December, 1984

ALL THE NEWS. The club bulletin was the written voice of CIAM. It was published monthly under the direction of Joseph Nadhir and Louis Stephen after the official grand opening of Southfield Manor on May 31, 1981. The first issue was only four pages; years later, it increased to 12 pages as other club members joined to help. The bulletin listed all the club functions and items of interest, including all activities, programs, board policies, and procedures. This is the front page of the 1984 bulletin. It was published in both English and Arabic. (Courtesy of Ralph Ayar.)

GET ON BOARD. When Southfield Manor opened its doors for the first time, the interim board of directors decided to call for an election of seven board members to care for club operations and management and to grow membership to 600. The first CIAM election for the newly built club made history as 35 people ran to fill those seven seats. This was a testimony to members' excitement, love, and dedication to serve. (Courtesy of Chaldean American Chamber of Commerce.)

SENATOR FOR THE PEOPLE. Southfield Manor was the home for all major events and community functions. State and US representatives were frequent visitors, whether dining with a friend or looking for campaign support. This practice continued at Shenandoah Country Club, which has been visited by every Michigan governor and Detroit mayor. Pictured at Southfield Manor are, from left to right, CIAM president Najib Karmo; N. Peter Antone; US senator Carl Levin, a true friend to the community who received the CIAM certificate of highest achievement and appreciation; and Dr. Talat Karmo. (Courtesy of Dr. Talat Karmo.)

REVISIONIST HISTORY. On September 14, 1989, the CIAM educational committee invited Dr. Benham Abu Alsouf, an Iraqi Cambridge graduate and professor at the University of Baghdad, to hold a lecture on "Mesopotamia and the Chaldeans." His talk was informative, enlightening, and very confusing! Unlike many historians, Alsouf claimed that Chaldeans and Assyrians are religious titles that are irrelevant and have no national identity. Many felt he was marginalizing minorities and playing to the tune of the Iraqi government. Seen here is Dave Nona (right), Jesuit College graduate and community activist, being interviewed about the talk by Zuhair Karmo from TV Orient, a Middle Eastern broadcasting company. (Courtesy of Dr. Talat Karmo.)

YOUTH, THE CAPITAL OF THE FUTURE. As the community established roots, people began to create social organizations and clubs, with the church hall as the center of activities and events. Chaldeans' ethnic heritage and religion were no longer the handicaps they might have been in Iraq. Men and women of diverse backgrounds worked together to build and grow their social organizations and clubs, emphasizing the permanence of their migration. (Courtesy of Sohail Dayimiya.)

NEW BLOOD. The Chaldean youth were the most important part of any religious, social, or cultural organization, injecting the new blood of active, educated, and hard-working individuals to help establish various community organizations. These happy young community members were involved in groups as diverse as the Chaldean Federation of America, Chaldean Youth, Associated Food Dealers, CIAM, and, serving the community since 1982, the Chaldean Voice, including Shoki Konja, Saher Yaldo, Fawzi Dalli, Danny Babi, and Maher Kanouna. (Courtesy of Sabah "Abo Nono" Isho.)

FASHION FORWARD. Established in 1961, the Chaldean American Ladies of Charity (CALC) are known to be "the most noble and compassionate example of community outreach," as Bryon Perry wrote in his book *The Chaldeans*. To celebrate their 40th anniversary in 2001, they held a fashion show showcasing regional clothing. That included the *abaya*, a black robe covering a woman's body from head to toe except her hands, feet, and face; the *kochma*, a head covering decorated with precious stones and beads worn mostly by the women of Telkaif; and the *hashimi*, a Baghdadi dress favored by upper-class society. Moving to fashion popular in America, more upscale dresses were on display, with designers like St. John and Herve Leger representing the Parisian style of molding the body into the perfect female form. (Both, courtesy of CALC.)

GOLFMANSHIP. Good conduct (fairness, respect for one's opponent, and graciousness in winning or losing) describes Doug Saroki, longtime club member and golfer, who took the lead to organize a parent-and-child golf camp at Ferris State University's Katke Golf Course in Big Rapids. Held in June 2001, the camp introduced golf to new players, allowed parents quality time with their children, and gave the kids the chance to make new friends. Shenandoah members were encouraged to take up the sport of American presidents. As PGA professional Mike Hodgins told attendees at the golf camp, "The key for the future of golf and for your club at Shenandoah is to keep your kids playing the game to be able to enjoy it." (Author's collection.)

EDUCATION FIRST. Occupational diversification has been occurring at a much faster pace than ever in the community. Most young American-born Chaldeans and some new immigrants have achieved college educations and are working as doctors, lawyers, engineers, accountants, and computer tech consultants, in addition to many other occupations. But the vast majority had, at one time, a tie to the grocery store business. (Courtesy of CALC.)

DIPLOMACY AT ITS BEST. Rend Al-Rahim was the first Iraqi ambassador to Washington after the American invasion of Iraq in 2003. She was the official voice of Iraq in America and the first woman to serve as a symbol of the country's new secular democracy. During her visit with the Chaldean community at Southfield Manor, she disregarded all diplomatic formalities by hugging and kissing everyone who greeted her. "I feel at home among members of my family and friends," she said. Ambassador Al-Rahim has more than one thing in common with the rest of the group in the picture: they are all Iraqi by birth, they all opposed Saddam Hussein and his regime, and they all retained their long-expired Iraqi passports. (Courtesy of Nabil Roumayah.)

CHARITY BEGINS AT HOME. On November 7, 1997, CALC—which always took the lead in helping others to make a difference—coordinated with many CIAM committees, including public relations, women, youth, and the management team, to raise funds to build a Chaldean senior living home. Pictured having a great time at the Millionaire Party at Southfield Manor are, from left to right facing the camera, Rosemary Bannon, Fr. Emmanuel Reyes, and Fr. Sarhad Jammo. (Courtesy of CALC.)

THE PATRIARCH IN TOWN. CIAM directors invited Patriarch Raphael Bidawid, along with Chaldean bishops, to a five-course dinner on August 13, 2002, with board members, committee chairs, and past presidents, to celebrate the ordination of Fr. Sarhad Jammo as the bishop of the new Diocese of St. Peter in the western United States. The patriarch started his short speech by saying "the food is delicious!" (His favorite was *kubba mosulia*, but he liked everything.) He thanked the club and management, commended the founding fathers, and urged the dedicated members to continue their hard work for the unity of the community. He also encouraged the attendees to embrace their new homeland of America and its values and principles. (Author's collection.)

DEDICATION, COMMITMENT, AND PRIDE. CALC honored Chaldean American US armed forces members for their dedication and patriotism with a special tribute on June 14, 2002. The gathering at Southfield Manor was an opportunity for future generations of Chaldeans to acknowledge the many priceless freedoms enjoyed every day. Serving in the armed forces gave the men a stronger sense of belonging in the United States, and social status as veterans upon their return. (Courtesy of CALC.)

PATRIARCH BIDAWID. On November 22, 1997, the CIAM board of directors had the honor of participating in this photo session with Patriarch Raphael Bidawid. He was visiting the United States to attend the signing of an agreement to consolidate the foundation of the Chaldean Catholic Church and Assyrian Church of the East. All past presidents, CIAM committee chairs, Chaldean clergy, and Chaldean sisters joined the visiting patriarch for a holy supper. From left to right are (first row, seated) Raad Kathawa, Michael George, Isam Yaldo, Bishop Ibrahim Ibrahim, Patriarch Raphael Bidawid, Bishop George Garmo, Bishop Hanna Zora, Bishop Gabriel Kassab, Rev. Edward Bikoma, and Rev. Emmanuel Reyes; (second row) Rev. Hanna Cheikho, Rev. Jerjis Ibrahim, Sr. Teresa Shikwana, Sr. Josephine Seman, Thaira Kathawa, Rev. Suleiman Denha, Rev. Benyamen Bethydegar, Rev. Zouhair Kejbou, Rev. Manuel Boji, Karim Toma, Kais Zair, Jacob Bacall, Anne Bacall, Faris Nalu, Vivian Nalu, Nancy Boji, Sr. Alena Jamil, Nasrin Bidawid, and Rev. Jacob Yasso; (third row) Randy Oram, Hind Oram, Hermiz Bidawid, Najib Karmo, Vivian Yaldo, Rosemary Antone, Zuhair Antone, Mohammad Ansari (Southfield Manor's general manager), Basima Ayar, Ralph Ayar, Rev. Sarhad Jammo, Jaklin Shina, Hanna Shina, Basil Boji, Sr. Clotelda Kinaya, Bushra Mansour, Dr. Jacob Mansour, unidentified, Sr. Ferial Qirma, Sr. Nada Khubeir, and Sr. Margaret Homa. (Courtesy of Isam Yaldo.)

CAREER DAY. CIAM, with CALC and the Chaldean American Bar Association, sponsored Career Day on April 19, 1997, at Southfield Manor. The event gave Chaldean students a chance to learn about various careers. More than 50 Chaldean professionals and businesspeople took time to meet and speak with the students. Two decades later, the number of Chaldean professionals has tripled and includes many working in the medical, engineering, accounting, and computer science fields. These represent the fabric of today's Chaldean society. (Courtesy of Dr. Talat Karmo.)

FAREWELL TO SOUTHFIELD MANOR. Construction of Shenandoah Country Club was in full swing, and the time had come to say goodbye to a facility that served the community for a quarter century. Southfield Manor was the site of more than 10,000 events. In 2003, the CIAAM board of directors asked Jacob Bacall to head a special advisory committee. In a 9-3 vote, they agreed to sell Southfield Manor. Landmark Brokerage Services, spearheaded by CIAAM member John Kello, handled the sale. After several bids were received, the board of directors decided to sell the manor to a non-competing business. In 2005, the club was sold to Comcast for $3,582,000, and all of the furniture, fixtures, and equipment was sold at auction. In June 2006, Comcast became the owner. From left to right are committee members Jamal Shallal, Adhid Miri, Faisal Arabo, Nabby Yono, Francis Boji, Jacob Bacall, Karim Toma, Shamil Halabu, and Raad Kathawa. (Courtesy of Karim Toma.)

Five

SHENANDOAH COUNTRY CLUB

UP FOR GRABS

Shenandoah was designed as a golf course by Jerry Matthews, and the first nine holes were built in 1950, with a plan to add another nine holes a few years later. Today, it is a picturesque par-72 at 6,500 yards. Shenandoah made the news when it constructed a modern clubhouse in 1966, moving from an old stone farmhouse. The grand opening of that facility was celebrated on June 12, 1968.

In 1989, CIAM acquired the Shenandoah Golf and Country Club. "It was not that easy to swing the undecided and ultra-conservative members of the club to vote in favor of purchasing Shenandoah for one simple reason," recalled Sharkey George, a longtime golfer and the older brother of Michael George. "The vast majority of our club members are not golfers."

More than a handful of influential club members were against the change. "You're getting 147 acres in the heart of Oakland County for a little over $4 million. It's a no-brainer!" Michael George said at a general membership meeting in July 1989. "If the general membership turns it down, I will buy it as a business opportunity."

A decade later, the purchase of Shenandoah turned out to be one of the best moves in the history of the organization. After all, it was a community dream since early 1943. Construction of the new Shenandoah clubhouse has attracted many young members and children to enjoy the numerous amenities the semi-private club has to offer, including athletic facilities, a members-only dining room, the more informal Mixed Grille, a large ballroom, an outdoor swimming pool, and the 18-hole golf course. In addition, Shenandoah is home to the new Chaldean Cultural Center museum.

The idea was documented in Article 2 of CIAM's certificate of incorporation on August 31, 1965: "to acquire and/or build a center for the community and its organization in order to serve their various functions to further the social and cultural affairs of its members."

SHENANDOAH GOLF AND COUNTRY CLUB ESTATES. The idea of Shenandoah started in the 1950s with the vision to build an 18-hole course (par-72, 6,500 yards) designed by Jerry Matthews. The vision included a park-like setting with lakes, mature trees, deer, and all kinds of birds. It would be a bit of beautiful northern Michigan right at one's Oakland County doorstep. This model gives a bird's-eye view of the proposed plan. (Courtesy of Bernard J. Wojnar and family.)

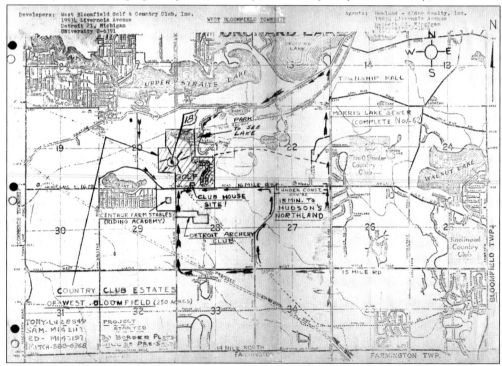

PRIDE AND PRESTIGE. This is an original design by W. Bruce Matthews, son of Jerry Matthews, and includes the clubhouse. The front nine holes were to be built in 1964. The design was to include a subdivision around the course. "I promoted the project of Shenandoah Golf and Country Estates as a symbol of pride and prestige," said the project developer of Shenandoah Golf Course and Estates. (Courtesy of Bernard J. Wojnar and family.)

TOP OF THE LINE. W. Bruce Matthews and son W. Bruce Matthews III designed an additional nine holes to be constructed at a later date. This image is a new rendering of the proposed clubhouse design by C.E. Noetzel. "Membership in the new Shenandoah Golf and Country Club is waiting for you," said Gordon Williamson, the development's marketing director. "Recreation and social facilities for the entire family!" The plan included a 29,000-square-foot, two-level building on a hillside, with each floor having access to ground level. The clubhouse was expected to be ready for the 1967 season chock-full of amenities: cocktail lounge, dining room, men's grill, ballroom, pro shop, club storage, and lockers, showers, and sauna for both men and women. (Courtesy of CIAAM files and records.)

A GRAND AFFAIR. Moving from an old stone farmhouse into a modern clubhouse with all the trimmings, Shenandoah celebrated its grand opening on June 29, 1968, with complimentary cocktails and hors d'oeuvres followed by a formal dinner dance and entertainment. It was a festive evening to remember for years to come. (Courtesy of Bernard J. Wojnar and family.)

Shenandoah Golf and Country Club
cordially invites you to attend the
Grand Opening Cocktail Party
Saturday, the twenty-ninth of June
nineteen hundred and sixty-eight
complimentary cocktails and hors d'oeuvres
from seven to eight-thirty o'clock
members only
———
the cocktail party will be followed by a
Dinner Dance
dinner at eight-thirty
fifteen dollars per couple
Dick Stockwell and his Orchestra
nine-thirty to one-thirty o'clock
reservations are for members only
prior to the twenty-second of June
after that date guests will be permitted
if space is available
dress optional
R.S.V.P. phone 682-4300

PART OF THE CLUB. Shenandoah members are pictured at the bar after a game of golf. The vast majority of Shenandoah's members were spectators, not golfers, and Shenandoah was designed to handle a maximum of about 12,000 spectators at one time. (Courtesy of Bernard J. Wojnar and family.)

HOLE	CHAMPIONSHIP YARDAGE	REGULAR YARDAGE	PAR				HANDICAP				YARDS	PAR
1	416	391	4				7				367	
2	491	475	5				3				461	
3	162	150	3				17				138	
4	511	501	5				1				492	
5	445	434	4				5				386	
6	407	371	4				11				366	
7	405	400	4				9				335	
8	218	161	3				15				149	
9	355	339	4				13				307	
Out	3410	3222	36								3001	36
10	422	398	4				6				375	
11	325	306	4				14				288	
12	365	346	4				10				328	
13	525	508	5				4				492	
14	337	325	4				12				314	
15	184	171	3				16				159	
16	570	551	5				2				533	
17	165	152	3				18				141	
18	398	382	4				8				369	
In	3291	3139	36								2999	36
Total	6701	6361	72								6000	76

5600 WALNUT LAKE ROAD. Established in the 1950s, the golf course and the surrounding estates were introduced as Shenandoah Golf Course and Estates when CIAM purchased the old, tired golf course in 1989. The directors decided early on to preserve and treasure the original name and history, but the street number changed from 5900 to 5600 Walnut Lake Road in beautiful West Bloomfield. (Both, courtesy of Bernard J. Wojnar and family.)

DECK WITH A VIEW. Admission to the golf course does not guarantee a seat, and usually spectators have a heck of a time trying to peer over shoulders and heads to see what is going on. Like most golf courses, Shenandoah was not designed with crowds in mind. (Only Augusta National in Georgia, home of the Masters, has reshaped its course so that spectators can see more of the action.) Seen here is a crowd of spectators and players during the Michigan Golf Classic championship on September 4–7, 1969, in front of Shenandoah's original 1968 clubhouse, which was demolished in 2002 and replaced with a much larger building. Both then and now, Shenandoah offers an amazing view from its beautiful terrace. (Both, courtesy of Bernard J. Wojnar and family.)

SPOTLIGHT ON SHENANDOAH. Shenandoah enjoyed the national spotlight from September 4 to 7, 1969, when it hosted the Michigan Golf Classic championship. Larry Ziegler, a mainstay of the senior tour, won the event, beating Homero Blancas in a playoff. It was Ziegler's first PGA tour victory. He defeated Blancas with a birdie on the second hole of a sudden-death playoff. It was shocking news when tournament supervisor George Walsh revealed that the sponsors did not have enough money to pay the pledged prize of at least $100,000. It went down in history as the prize that was promised but never delivered. (Above, courtesy of Bernard J. Wojnar and family; below, courtesy of CIAAM files and records.)

UP FOR GRABS. "Did you know the golf course, the one right in the heart of one of the most affluent communities in Oakland County with 147 acres of land, is up for grabs? How can you go wrong, Mike?" Sharkey George asked his brother Mike George in his Livonia-based Melody Farms Dairy office. "But Chaldeans are not golfers, Sharkey," Mike responded with a shrug. "Well, just like everything else in life, there is always a first time. Sooner than later the golf bug will catch up with them. It is only a matter of time," Sharkey said. Pictured here from left to right are golf buddies Zuhair Antone, Ronnie Jamil, Sharkey George, and Faris Nalu. (Author's collection.)

BUYING SHENANDOAH. On April 3, 1989, the members of CIAM authorized the board of directors to negotiate the purchase of Shenandoah Country Club. On July 14, 1989, a letter from CIAM was sent to all members advising them of the fact that a purchase agreement to buy the 147-acre property was executed at $4.2 million, that due diligence was underway, and that Mike George had spoken to a couple of bankers to secure financing. (Courtesy of Bernard J. Wojnar and family.)

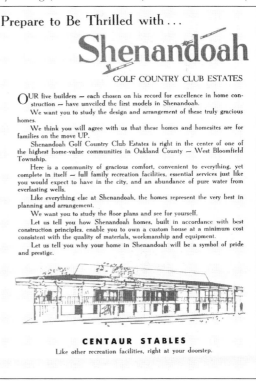

Prepare to Be Thrilled with . . .

Shenandoah
GOLF COUNTRY CLUB ESTATES

OUR five builders — each chosen on his record for excellence in home construction — have unveiled the first models in Shenandoah.

We want you to study the design and arrangement of these truly gracious homes.

We think you will agree with us that these homes and homesites are for families on the move UP.

Shenandoah Golf Country Club Estates is right in the center of one of the highest home-value communities in Oakland County — West Bloomfield Township.

Here is a community of gracious comfort, convenient to everything, yet complete in itself — full family recreation facilities, essential services just like you would expect to have in the city, and an abundance of pure water from everlasting wells.

Like everything else at Shenandoah, the homes represent the very best in planning and arrangement.

We want you to study the floor plans and see for yourself.

Let us tell you how Shenandoah homes, built in accordance with best construction principles, enable you to own a custom house at a minimum cost consistent with the quality of materials, workmanship and equipment.

Let us tell you why your home in Shenandoah will be a symbol of pride and prestige.

CENTAUR STABLES
Like other recreation facilities, right at your doorstep.

Chaldean-Iraqi Association of Michigan

EDITORIAL STAFF
Francis Boji
Jamal Shallal   Amir Denha
Dhafir Nona   Basil Najar
Talat Karmo   Louie Stephen

NEWS BULLETIN

Published for, and in the interest of, The Chaldean-Iraqi Association of Michigan

Bulk Mail
U.S. Postage
PAID
Permit No. 444
Southfield, MI

25626 Telegraph Road, Southfield, Michigan 48034 • Phone (313) 352-9020   **VOL. IX, NO. 5**   **AUG./SEPT. 1989**

PRESIDENT'S CORNER

Shenandoah Country Club: Fact or Fiction?

I am amazed at the reaction of the members of Southfield Manor and/or the Chaldean Community as it applies to the purchase of Shenandoah Country Club.

There was a general membership meeting on April 3, 1989 in which the members authorized the Board of Directors to negotiate the purchase of Shenandoah Country Club. There was no other communication except for the letter that was sent to all members dated July 14, 1989 advising them of the fact that we had executed purchase agreements. In the interim, before and after the letter was sent, certain members have related to uninterested parties their perception of what's going to happen at Shenandoah Country Club even though we have not finalized a master plan.

The rumors are rampage. Everyone seems to know more about Shenandoah Country Club than the Board of Directors.

If you as members visualize something better than my letter indicated, please call me directly. We welcome your recommendations and will support you if your ideas are conducive to the goals of the Chaldean Community.

Don't make a statement unless you are totally knowledgeable of the facts as to what we are proposing for the golf course and cultural center.

Conversations without substance can only cause more apprehension by outsiders and will arouse them to be opponents rather than allies. I can assure you that the Board of Directors and the majority of the members are dedicated to building a facility that will enhance the image of our community with social and recreational activities.

"A civilization cannot be destroyed from without until it is infested with false RUMORS and innuendos from within."

Author: Michael J. George

MICHAEL J. GEORGE

A LETTER FROM THE PRESIDENT. On July 14, 1989, Pres. Michael George wrote to all CIAM members addressing the new club purchase in English and Arabic. He covered the issues of concern and outlined the roadmap to build a Chaldean center while maintaining a public golf course. George offered his personal guarantee without any reservation and extended the invitation to other club members to participate in the guarantee of the loan. Manuel Meram joined as co-guarantor. By Christmas 1989, CIAM took ownership of Shenandoah Country Club and Golf Course. (Courtesy of CIAAM files and records.)

SCENIC BUT TOUGH. In 1993, CIAM added a driving range, putting green, and practice sand traps. Course improvement is part of CIAAM's budget, so it can compete with others in Oakland County. "This 18-hole course provides the best of both worlds," said Jim Neagals, Shenandoah's general manager and director of golf (pictured), in the April 27, 1996, *Observer and Eccentric.* (Author's collection.)

HAPPY FIRST COMMUNION. The original Shenandoah was a place for various community and public functions, including weddings, first communions, baptisms, and golf outings. These contributed greatly to the early survival of the newly purchased golf course. But that first Shenandoah banquet hall was perhaps most famous for its enormous cement columns spread throughout, as seen above in 1993 at Lauren Elizabeth Bacall's first holy communion, and below in a photograph of another communion held at Shenandoah Country Club. (Both, author's collection.)

West Bloomfield Eccentric

Your hometown newspaper serving West Bloomfield, Orchard Lake, Keego Harbor and the Lakes area for 28 years

ober 21, 2001 · www.observerandeccentric.com · 75¢

West Bloomfield, Michigan · ©2001 HomeTown Communications Network

Chaldean cultural center approved

BY DAN WEST
STAFF WRITER
dwest@oe.homecomm.net

The Western Hemisphere's first Chaldean cultural center is coming to West Bloomfield.

After five-and-a-half hours of intense scrutiny from planning commission and wetland board members Thursday, the Shenandoah Country Club was given the green light for an expansion and renovation project that features extensive landscaping, a 750-person banquet hall and a public cultural center.

After a planning commission vote approved the site plan at 12:34 a.m. Friday, about 30 Chaldeans remaining in the audience smiled, raised their arms and applauded the legal clear-

WEST BLOOMFIELD

ance for their "new home."

Jacob Bacall, president of the Chaldean Iraqi-American Association of Michigan, admitted he was pleasantly surprised.

"I'm excited," he said. "We've been

working on this for four years; it's k of like having a baby born."

With some planning commission absent due to family illnesses, only f of the nine board members were hand Thursday. After sorting o issues regarding drainage, wetlan traffic and size of the building, t

Please see CENTER,

Officials to face recall Tuesday

See related editorial, page A5

BY SUSAN B. TAUBER
STAFF WRITER
stauber@oe.homecomm.net

Sue Doyle and Eileen Seabolt were elected to the Keego Harbor City Council last Nov. 7. They've served 11 of their 36-month terms.

They'll find out Tuesday if city voters will allow them to stay in office for another two years.

Voters headed to the polls in Keego Harbor will decide whether to recall

Sue Doyle

Fall haul

STAFF PHOTO BY JERRY ZOLY

Leafy spray: *Groundskeeper Antonio Silva-Perez kicks up quite a cloud as he sweeps leaves at Pi*

OH, WHAT A NIGHT. The night of October 18, 2001, was dramatic and sobering, as the time came to vote on plans for a 90,000-square-foot clubhouse designed by Victor Saroki. An intense debate went on for five and a half hours before the votes were cast: Debra Davis, yes; Steve Budaj, no; Nancy Reed, no; Anne Jardou, yes; and Larry Brown, yes. The motion passed at 12:47 a.m. on Friday, October 19, 2001. "Everyone clapped, yelled and cried 'we made it!' " said Mary Dabish, the daughter of Sam Dabish, one of the original CIA members in 1943 and author of *The History of the Iraqi Community in America.* (Author's collection.)

Six

SHENANDOAH
GROUND BREAKING AND GROWTH

The Chaldean Iraqi American Association of Michigan (CIAAM) maintains the mother superior role over the rest of the community organizations in the United States. Since its inception in 1943, the organization has had the largest Chaldean family-based membership with established initiation fees and annual dues, a true testament to its value to members and its very existence. It is remarkable to realize that the membership is now in its fourth generation.

At the most recent general membership meeting on November 7, 2017, CIAAM reported that paid membership had reached 1,037 members, with $1.4 million collected in annual dues.

When the Chaldean Iraqi Association of Michigan (as it was known before the word "American" was added to the name in 2000) took over the ownership and operation of Shenandoah Country Club in December 1989, the property was in poor shape, having been neglected for some time.

The board's first decision was to close Shenandoah immediately and start a $1 million renovation to give it a good facelift. When the club opened on June 9, 1990, CIAM signed a new agreement with Shenandoah Country Club Inc. to lease the renovated facility for yearly rent of $630,000 payable in four equal installments on the first of January, April, July, and October.

The much-anticipated and long-awaited ground breaking for the new Shenandoah Country Club and, years later, the Chaldean Cultural Center, represent much more than members' financial success. It is a true reflection of the maturity and prosperity of virtually the entire Chaldean community in Michigan and abroad.

Many Chaldeans stepped up to help navigate Shenandoah Country Club during the economic meltdown of 2008–2009. First was Bishop Ibrahim Ibrahim, who said, "I will sell one of my 13 churches before losing Shenandoah." This was a very strong statement for the spiritual leader, who was filling the role of a community leader as well. Another club member, real estate developer Arkan Jonna, used his ingenuity and patience to make the best deal possible. Others who helped in the process included Louie Boji, Mike George, Neb Mekani, John Loussia, Jason Alkamano, Burt Kassab, Michael Sarafa, Raad Kathawa, Najib Samona, Francis Boji, Jacob Bacall, and Martin Manna. Each deserves more than a word of thanks.

"I take tremendous pride in saying I am a proud fourth-generation CIAAM member," said Blake George. "My great-great-grandfather, Tom George, was a CIAAM founding member. I am honored to carry membership number 235, which was passed to me by my grandfather, Michael J. George, just before he passed away in 2014."

Today, CIAAM is entering a new era. Operating revenue is doing extremely well, and the Chaldean Cultural Center museum finally opened to the public in October 2017. Shenandoah is the premier gathering spot for all four generations of the community, a place to share with family and friends, and a true house of Chaldeans.

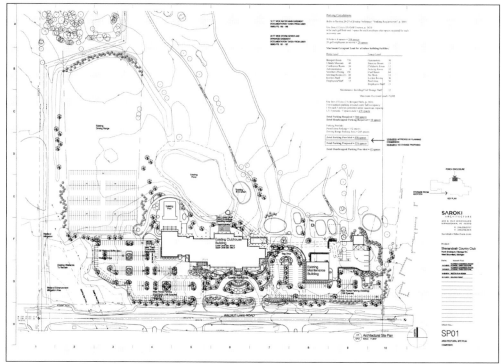

A Detailed Plan. The members of the club and its elected board of directors decided to work on the greater plan of building a Chaldean community center, which had been the top objective of CIAM since its founding. The first step was to form a committee, which after nearly three years came up with the most suitable design for a facility to engage all three generations at a community home-away-from-home. The 22 members of the Shenandoah Country Club planning committee submitted their report of recommendations to the CIAAM board in May 2002. Highlights included a project cost of $18,912,000 (a figure reached after consulting with Plante and Moran, one of the nation's largest certified public accounting and business advisory firms) and the recommendation to hire a construction manager rather than a general manager to build the new Shenandoah Country Club and Chaldean Cultural Center. The Shenandoah Country Club planning committee members were Francis Boji, Michael George, Zuhair Antone, Robert Kato, Riyadh Jiddou, Eliya Boji, Jamal Shallal, Carol Loussia, Charlie Semaan, Hikmat Zeer, Matthew Jonna, Victor Saroki, Tom George, Faris Nalu, Dhafir Nona, Sabah Summa, Nabby Yono, Raad Kathawa, Josephine Kassab, Isam Yaldo, Nizar Yono, and Jacob Bacall. (Courtesy of Victor Saroki.)

MORE THAN A DREAM.
The projected cost of the new Shenandoah Country Club and Chaldean Cultural Center was nearly $19 million. The board of directors gave unanimous approval to put the issue to a vote of the general membership. The document at right gives a detailed breakdown of the costs; below is an architectural rendering of the north elevation. (Both, author's collection.)

Building and construction costs	$14,226,966
Architects fees	800,000
Engineering/ surveying	100,000
All fees and Bond allowance	400,000
Financing costs	251,250
Capitalized construction interest	1,292,209
Total construction costs	$17,070,425
Furniture and fixtures	$ 750,474
Kitchen equipment	803,950
Audiovisual, alarm, data, telephone systems	150,000
Point of sale computer system	150,000
Total facility costs	18,924,849

We summarize the above numbers as follows:

1. Average cost of building per square foot Including
   All engineering And Fees   90,000 X $172.24 = $15,501,600.00

2. Cost of furniture, Kitchen
   Equipment and other   90,000 X $20.49 = $ 1,844,100.00

3. Financing costs and other
   Miscellaneous items   90,000 X $17.27 = $ 1,554,300.00

   TOTAL COST = $18,900,000.00

   Or   90,000,000 X $210.00 = $18,900,000.00

3

SHENANDOAH COUNTRY CLUB
AND
CHALDEAN CULTURAL CENTER
WEST BLOOMFIELD, MICHIGAN
VICTOR SAROKI & ASSOCIATES ARCHITECTS PC

YAYS AND NAYS. July 24, 2002, was a night to remember. Members were notified of a special general membership meeting to cast their historic vote for the new Shenandoah Country Club project. Brief presentations were given by club president Jacob Bacall, project architect Victor Saroki, planning and finance committee chairman Francis Boji, and the finance committee. At first, the atmosphere was somewhat reserved, but then it became cautiously optimistic. As decision time neared to embrace the recommendations of the experts and volunteers, the motion was made to build a new Shenandoah Country Club and Chaldean Cultural Center at the cost of nearly $19 million to replace the old Shenandoah building at 5600 Walnut Lake Road in West Bloomfield. Completion was projected for 2004. By an overwhelming margin, the motion passed with 236 for, 19 against, and 2 undecided. (Author's collection.)

CHOOSING A CONTRACTOR. Several qualified and well-known contractors bid to build the community center with a budget of around $19 million. The five final contenders were Walbridge Aldinger, Frank Rewold and Son, Parlovecchio Building Company, Kalabat Construction, and Jonna Construction Company. Bids were submitted between December 19, 2001, and January 16, 2002. For a while, it seemed that the contract was slipping away from Jonna Construction Company, which worried some members of the selection committee. But, as a member of the planning committee and the board of directors, the author witnessed that the guidelines for selection were followed. Price or size was not the principal issue. It merely came down to one thing: if a dispute arose, which of the contractors would be willing to settle the matter without going to court? Who would be the one to safeguard the interest of CIAAM? Jonna was the right and obvious choice. (Both, author's collection.)

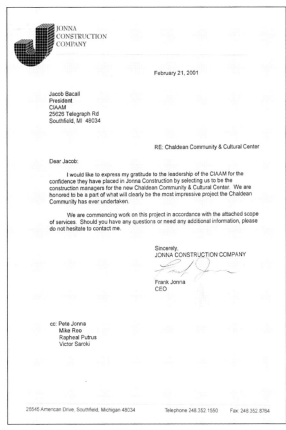

FINALLY, IT IS HERE. A new generation of Chaldeans was inspired by the kickoff of a $19-million project with a cultural center and museum that would serve as a library and exhibition facility to increase awareness and knowledge of the Chaldean American community locally, nationally, and internationally. Pictured here is community leader Sharkey Haddad proudly holding the proposed community center brochure, along with his daughter Sindel. (Author's collection.)

DIGGING IN. The ground-breaking ceremony took place beneath a tent on the green of the old 18th hole. CIAAM members, guests, dignitaries, speakers, and media were all invited. The CIAAM awards committee presented four ceremonial shovels to the CIAAM president, two bishops, and Michigan lieutenant governor Dick Posthumus. They were emblazoned with the CIAAM emblem featuring the Lion of Babylon as a symbol of Chaldean might and glory. Interlink Media organized the event. (Author's collection.)

A Festive Day. At 4:30 on the afternoon of October 10, 2002, the ground-breaking program started with beautiful Middle Eastern music by Albert Matloub. Master of ceremonies Michael Sarafa welcomed the assembled media, dignitaries, and guests. Speakers included Oakland County commissioner Shelley Goodman Taub, state house Democratic leader Samuel "Buzz" Thomas, state representative Marc Shulman, and Michigan lieutenant governor Dick Posthumus (right), who spoke about the many positive qualities of the Chaldean community and its positive impact on the state. Below, from left to right, are Samuel "Buzz" Thomas, Tony Antone, Marc Shulman, Dick Posthumus, Louie Boji, West Bloomfield Township supervisor David Flaisher, West Bloomfield trustee Stuart Brickner, Fuad Manna, Asma Halabu, and Dr. Shakib Halabu. (Both, author's collection.)

HISTORY IN THE MAKING. "*Yoma tarikhinaya ta uma dee ian kildaya*," said CIAAM president Jacob Bacall in Aramaic, which translates to "it's a historical day for the Chaldean people." He added, "The new facility will be a source of pride and glory for many generations to come." If Chaldeans had their own country, he noted, Shenandoah would be its White House. The ceremony was like a big Chaldean wedding, complete with a *zeffa*, the joyful communal dance celebrating a bride and groom. Due to the heavy presence of priests, two bishops, and a large group of Chaldean sisters, the only thing missing was a belly dancer. October 10, 2002, marked another milestone for the Chaldean community. (Both, author's collection.)

PRIDE AND JOY. This was not just an ordinary Thursday for members of the Chaldean community. The blessing of lovely weather inspired true joy in the many attendees. Here was the fulfillment of the community dream. On hand to honor the occasion were all the past presidents of CIAAM. Among those pictured here are Buzz Thomas, Francis Boji, Johnny Karmo, Dick Posthumus, Bishop Ibrahim Ibrahim, Faris Nalu, Marc Shulman, Jacob Bacall, Bishop Sarhad Jammo, Jamal Shallal, Mike Khami, and Najib Ayar. (Both, author's collection.)

PROUD TO BE HERE. A huge tent was installed to accommodate the many invited guests on local and state levels, CIAAM members, and local and statewide media to cover the event on television, radio, newspapers, and magazines. Pictured here are the Chaldean sisters and officials from West Bloomfield Township along with other CIAAM members. (Author's collection.)

BRIGHT FUTURE. Not long after the opening of Southfield Manor in 1981, the general membership realized that there was not much to offer the younger generation. When the opportunity to buy Shenandoah became available, diligent and visionary CIAAM members pushed hard to make it happen. Their persistence paid off in the end. More than half of CIAAM's current members were not yet born or too young to remember Southfield Manor's early years of operation. (Author's collection.)

WORTH THE WAIT. Omar Jarbou, the local famous *zorna* player, along with his drummer, led the guests to the clubhouse. Guests arrived indoors to two open bars and a video presentation detailing the club's amenities. The dance floor was taken over by about 400 seats, nine round tables, and 15 high-tops. Soft Middle Eastern music played in the background after the live music was completed. The hall was decorated with flowers, and pictures of all the Chaldean villages of Iraq were hung throughout. (Both, author's collection.)

COMING ATTRACTIONS. A 20-minute video took guests on a virtual walk-through of all 90,000 square feet of what was to come. This included the banquet hall seating up to 700 people, private dining room area, swimming pool, gymnasium, basketball court, Mixed Grille, meeting and activity rooms, and administrative offices, along with a peek at the upcoming Chaldean Cultural Center. (Both, author's collection.)

MA BASEEMA (HOW JOYFUL)! After the video presentation, an abundance of food was served throughout the hall. The offerings included every kind and type of food and dessert that could be found on the Southfield Manor menu, accompanied by Chaldean folk music and dance. (Author's collection.)

ALL IN THE FAMILY. Southfield Manor employees and operating staff became their own extended family. Twice, employees found their match and started a new life together! Others became close friends both on and off the job. Pictured here is Southfield Manor's general manager accompanied by his staff at the Shenandoah ground-breaking celebration. (Author's collection.)

BUILDING A DREAM. Seen here is Birmingham architect Victor Saroki, who designed Shenandoah. He employed what he called a "clay brick of Babylon look" for Shenandoah and the use of energy-efficient, environmentally friendly products. (Author's collection.)

TIRELESS VOLUNTEERS. The planning committee became the construction committee, and one of its many tasks was to award and verify all submitted bids and approved change orders. The committee's professionalism and dedication were at the heart of seeing the long-awaited dream slowly come to life. The eight members of the construction committee are, from left to right, (seated) Raad Kathawa, Ed Miri, and Najib Samona; (standing) Jamal Shallal, Isam Yaldo, Faris Nalu, Francis Boji, and Jacob Bacall. (Raad Kathawa.)

VIPs. Yonadam Yowsup Kanna, a leader of Zowaa, the Assyrian Democratic party in Iraq, was part of the Iraq Governing Council in 2003. A private lunch was held in his honor when he and other Zowaa members visited the new Shenandoah in 2004. CIAAM president Ed Miri gave the visitors a tour of the building and its compounds. "It's absolutely magnificent, and we should be proud of such a beautiful landmark," said the guest, pictured above at center in first row with other Zowaa members in the private members' dining room during construction. (Both, author's collection.)

THE FIRST OF MANY. As the number of immigrant families increased, their hard work led to increased financial wellbeing and a higher standard of living and enjoyment of life. The need for a bigger and greater banquet facility became obvious as more and more people grew out of the smaller spaces offered by social houses and churches. Shown here is Shenandoah's very first wedding—Nadir and Monica Kizi celebrated their nuptials on January 9, 2005. (Courtesy of Nadir and Monica Kizi.)

GOOD BUSINESS. Wedding parties as large as 1,000 guests were once the norm, but today, receptions of 400 to 500 people have become more common. Wedding parties and other special events are big business at Shenandoah. Just as at Southfield Manor, banquet revenue accounts for more than 50 percent of the food business and has been the biggest profit source for the association since its inception. (Author's collection.)

GIVING A NEIGHBOR A HELPING HAND. After sorting out issues including drainage, wetlands, traffic, and the size of the building, debate arose over parking during the site plan approval in October 2002. Temple Israel offered the use of its parking lot to help Shenandoah overcome the township's concern of adequate parking, and the same courtesy applies to Temple Israel if needed. It truly has been a good, strong relationship between the two neighbors. (Courtesy of CIAAM files and records.)

Temple Israel

5725 WALNUT LAKE ROAD, WEST BLOOMFIELD, MICHIGAN 48323-2373
(248) 661-5700 • FAX: (248) 661-1302

ROBERT J. GORDON
PRESIDENT

July 27, 2007

The Shenandoah Board of Directors
c/o Mr. Michael Sarafa, President
5600 Walnut Lake Road
West Bloomfield, MI 48323

Dear Michael:

On behalf of the Temple Israel Board of Trustees, I would like to personally thank you and the entire Shenandoah leadership for opening your doors and welcoming us into the Country Club and the Chaldean Community Center. You must be very proud of such a meaningful legacy. I know we were honored that you shared it with us.

Thank you again for hosting this wonderful dinner and tour. We are proud to have you as neighbors and hope that our common concerns continue to unite us in the future.

Sincerely,

Robert J. Gordon
President

RJG:kkm

ROOM WITH A VIEW. Shenandoah's dining room and its large adjacent terrace offer scenic, panoramic views of the golf course. Since opening in 2005, the dining room has made history by hosting highly placed dignitaries and well-known international figures. Special guests have included 2008 presidential candidate Mitt Romney, US vice president Joe Biden, longtime US senator John McCain, and Iraqi prime minister Ibrahim Al-Jaafari. (Author's collection.)

RIBBON-CUTTING DAY. It took almost three years to build the club, and the final cost was around $24 million, not counting the purchase price of $4.2 million for the original building and land and the subsequent renovation of $1 million. The $5 million overrun was higher than the construction industry's national average of 8 to 15 percent, attributed by most to upgrades and change orders. Among those cutting the ribbon on July 25, 2005, were instrumental community leader Mike George (third from left), the CIAAM board of directors, and Comerica Bank chairman and chief executive officer Ralph W. Babb Jr. (second from left). (Author's collection.)

PAYING TRIBUTE. The original members of the Chaldean Iraqi Association did not live long enough to witness a bit of history with the grand opening of Shenandoah. But the new club includes many traditional details of the past, including the use of brick and stone in homage to the ancient Ishtar Gate. While the club is privately owned by the community, the 18-hole golf course and lavish banquet hall are open to the public, and millions of dollars have been spent to keep them in magnificent condition. (Author's collection.)

HONORING THE OLD GUARD. In 2006, senior club members were honored for their loyalty, dedication, and service for many decades. They each contributed a tremendous amount of time to make the club what it is today. They enjoy the fruit of their hard labor. From left to right are (first row, seated) Karim Sarafa, Sharkey George, Thomas Denha, Sami Kassab, and Dr. Jamil Antone; (second row, standing) Jacob Bacall, Raad Kathawa, Salman Sesi, Ralph Ayar, and Adhid Miri. (Courtesy of Dounia Senawi-Lievan.)

THIS CLUB WILL BE SAVED! During the economic meltdown of 2008–2009, Ibrahim Ibrahim, the Chaldean bishop of the eastern United States, paid very close attention to the club's financial crisis. He made the decision to lend the club $500,000 to keep it floating as things turned sour and the turbulence reached its highest level of emergency belt-tightening measures. Mar Ibrahim came to the podium at a general membership meeting in 2009 and said in a firm and decisive voice, "This club will be saved, even if we have to sell one of our churches." The club was saved through the hard work and goodwill of diehard members. (Author's collection.)

GROUND LEVEL OF MODESTY. The Mixed Grille, which sits in the lower level near the pro shop, is a casual spot where members and golfers can enjoy a relaxed atmosphere. Almost immediately after Shenandoah's grand opening on July 25, 2005, a massive reconfiguration and retrofitting of the lower level was undertaken to please a group of members who felt deprived and degraded by being confined to a room with limited windows and only a glimpse of the sun and fresh air. A sum of $1.5 to $1.8 million was spent to satisfy a handful of old comrades and loyalists. (Author's collection.)

VIRTUES OF HOSPITALITY. Guests invited to dine at Shenandoah can always be assured of a healthy and high-quality meal. Many of the authentic recipes and centuries-old culinary traditions emphasize the generous use of vegetables, a moderate amount of meat, and a variety of spices. Pictured here is Najib Samona (fourth from left) with his guest from Iraq, Dr. Mothanna Al-Hoory (sixth from left), who both taught at Al-Mustansiriya University in the 1970s. They are joined by a group of friends enjoying a feast of traditional Iraqi food. (Author's collection.)

THINKING AHEAD. Long before CIAM decided to purchase Shenandoah, community leaders discovered that the participation of the younger generation at club activities was basically zero. To remedy that, these visionary minds added a variety of amenities to the club, including a large outdoor swimming pool, a gym for basketball and volleyball, and golf leagues to encourage young players. "We want a place so our young ones can enjoy our heritage together, much like the Jewish Community Center," said Michael George to the *Detroit Free Press* in July 1989 regarding the purchase of Shenandoah Country Club (SCC). Pictured above are some first-generation Chaldean Americans born between 1980 and 1985 who are all proud club members today. From left to right are (first row) Lauren Bacall, Derrick Bacall, Monica Bacall (Zeer), and Angela Bacall (Jaboro); (second row) Steven Bacall, Mark Bacall, and Christina Bacall (Oraha). Pictured below is a typical summer day at SCC's pool. (Both, author's collection.)

The Look Says it All. News of the economic meltdown of 2008 and 2009 worried everyone in America, young and old alike. The concern of being in the negative got every member worried about the future of the newly built home. These lifelong friends cherish the good times they spend in each other's company, but the fear of losing the club was real. From left to right are Sidky Sadik and his friends Abdu-ahad Aboodi and Sabah Bahnam. (Author's collection.)

Years of Struggle. During the economic downturn, devoted club members like Basim Shina and his brothers, the late John Loussia, and Nick Sandiha and his family loaned $200,000 to $300,000 to cover the monthly operations. The funds were repaid a week or two later. It was still unclear what was to come. (Author's collection.)

Operating Agreement
of
Shenandoah Investors, LLC

Prepared By:

SESI & SESI, P.C.
ATTORNEYS AT LAW

RAMY J. SESI
32000 Northwestern Highway, Suite 155
Farmington Hills, Michigan 48334
248.626.5050 phone ● 248.626.5757 fax
www.sesilaw.com
ramy.sesi@sesilaw.com

A limited liability company formed in the State of Michigan

THE RESCUERS. The new SCC was under tremendous pressure to raise $7 million to pay off the final settlement with Charter One Bank. A local private bank agreed to loan CIAAM $3 million with commissions, but CIAAM first had to raise the initial amount of at least $3.5 million from its members before asking the outside lender to match it. Second, a personal guarantee of $1 million was needed as backup assurance. Third, a first lien was placed on the SCC property. More than $3 million was raised by less than 30 CIAAM members to save the sinking ship, and the loan was paid off on the last day of the calendar year in 2009. The rescuers were Nadia Atisha, Francis Boji, Louie Boji, Ronnie Farida, Terry Farida, Sam Haddad, Arkan Jonna, Frank Jonna, John Loussia, Hani Mio, Najib Samona, Basil Shina, Mazin Shina, Mike Shina, Jacob Bacall, Rodney George, Fadi Hakim, Freddie Loussia, Nick Sandiha, Steve Salim Yaldoo, Eddie Yaldo, Faiq Konja, Sahir Gappy, Bobby Hesano, Audie Jabero, and Jamal Qonja. (Courtesy of CIAAM files and records.)

[Signature page to Limited Guaranty]

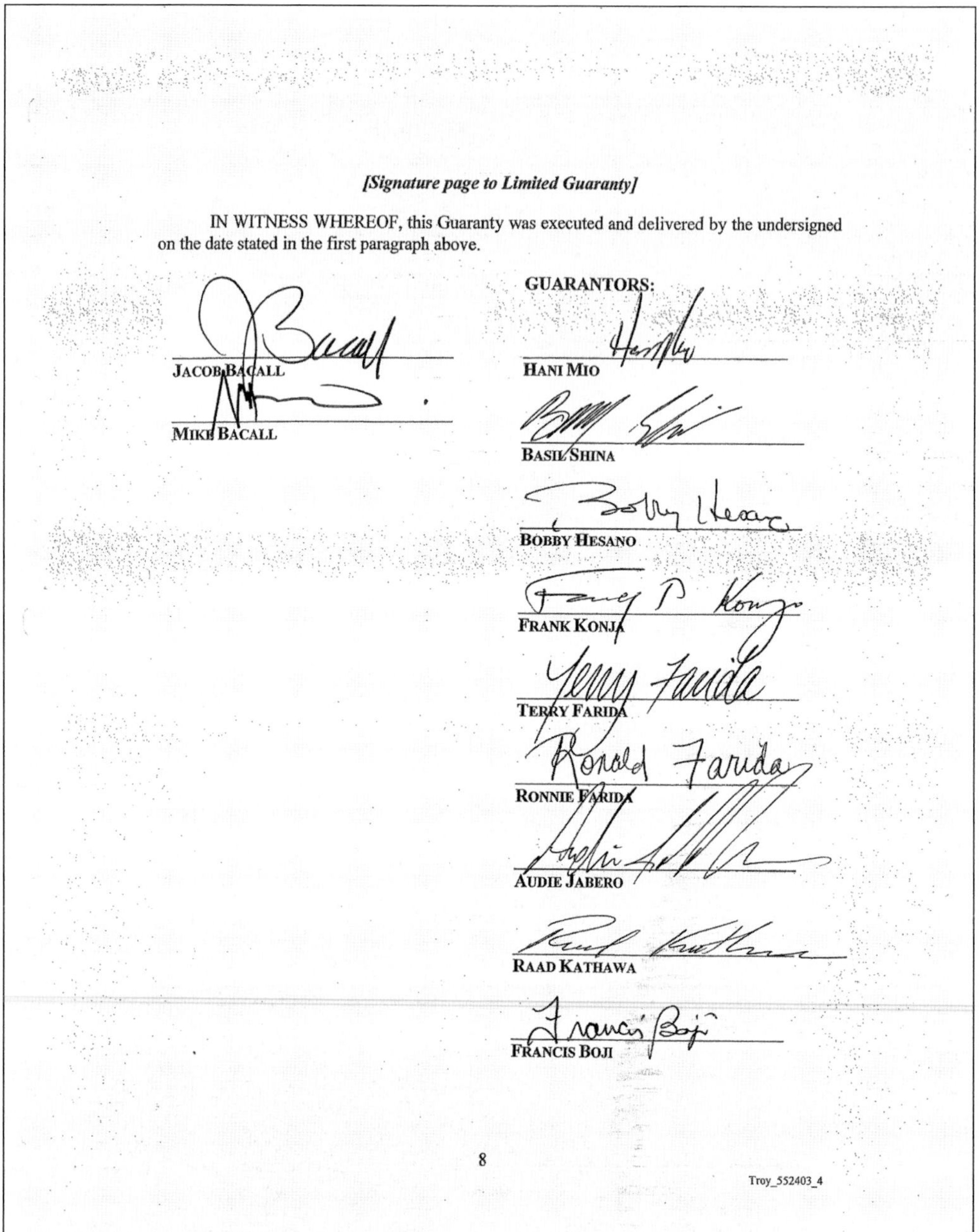

IN WITNESS WHEREOF, this Guaranty was executed and delivered by the undersigned on the date stated in the first paragraph above.

GUARANTORS:

JACOB BACALL

MIKE BACALL

HANI MIO

BASIL SHINA

BOBBY HESANO

FRANK KONJA

TERRY FARIDA

RONNIE FARIDA

AUDIE JABERO

RAAD KATHAWA

FRANCIS BOJI

8

Troy_552403_4

Shouldering the Burden. To solve the club's financial crisis in 2009, bank loan approval imposed the condition that $1 million be personally guaranteed. The following members agreed that the bank could have immediate recourse against the guarantors of action if necessary: Hani Mio ($50,000), Basim Shina ($125,000), Bobby Hesano ($75,000), Frank Konja ($75,000), Terry Farida ($75,000), Ronnie Farida ($75,000), Audie Jabero ($75,000), Raad Kathawa ($200,000), Francis Boji ($100,000), Jacob Bacall ($100,000), and Mike Bacall ($50,000). (Courtesy of CIAAM files and records.)

SHISH KABOB, THE HAMBURGER OF CHALDEANS. Hands down, shish kabob is the most popular dish in Iraq, as it was in Mesopotamia during medieval times. It is the equivalent of hamburgers to Americans. The word "kabob" was used throughout history for both the skewered grilled pieces of meat and the long, flattened, skewered, ground meat. Here, chef of all chefs and current general manager Lee Sharkas (right) and his head chef Larry Wood cradle the dish for which Shenandoah is well known. (Photograph by Janeau Deese.)

QUAIL IN POMEGRANATE MOLASSES. One of Shenandoah's amazingly delicious and unique dishes is quail, grown on a country farm in Northern Michigan. Cooked with caramelized onions and sizzled with pomegranate molasses to perfection, it has just the right balance of sweet and nutty flavors. Quail may be split in half before cooking on the grill or stovetop and has been a signature dish since the early days of Southfield Manor in the early 1980s. (Photograph by Janeau Deese.)

EARLY BIRDS. Eating dinner after 10:00 p.m. is a common Middle Eastern tradition. But the routine has changed as Chaldean immigrants integrate into American life, and many members and their guests now dine between 6:00 and 8:00 p.m. Food is served late, followed by tea and homemade pastries or local traditional sweets such as baklava, *zlabia*, or *buxom*. Back home, Chaldeans still eat closer to midnight and less formally, while here in the United States, it is earlier and more formal. (Author's collection.)

CHOOSING MICHIGAN. Despite falling rates of immigration in America between 2000 and 2012, largely the result of the 2008 global economic crisis, Michigan ranked second only behind California in attracting Iraqis. Remarkably, 92 percent of recent immigrant Chaldeans selected Michigan as their destination, according to Data Driven Detroit in a 2016 issue of *DBusiness* magazine. Picture here is Fr. Douglas Bazi, visiting from Erbil, Iraq, and US senator Debbie Stabenow of Michigan. (Author's collection.)

ALSO A PLACE OF MOURNING. Just as with Southfield Manor, CIAAM members utilize their home base at Shenandoah for a variety of social and religious functions. Lately, Shenandoah has been the frequent site of *ta'azia*, a funeral gathering where people can pay their respects to families who have lost a loved one. Pictured is a 2016 ta'azia held in Shenandoah's activity hall. (Author's collection.)

CELEBRATIONS FOR ALL. It was decided at a very early stage of planning that the new Shenandoah had to keep up with the increasing demand for banquet business in the Oakland County area. Shenandoah took all the necessary measures to add a kosher kitchen to meet the dietary needs of observant Jews. It also revamped the kitchen to accommodate Indian clients and guests. (Courtesy of CIAAM files and records.)

THE ART OF BELLY DANCING. A short time after Shenandoah opened, many types of classes were offered, including belly dancing taught by professional Middle Eastern dancers. To enroll, one just needed to wear comfortable clothes along with a hip belt or scarf. A few members joined the class, but not enough to keep it on the permanent schedule, unlike the golf lessons, which are always offered. Pictured is a private event in the ballroom in 2005. (Author's collection.)

HIGH SPIRITS. As much as dancing is an art, it is also a fun and important part of any wedding. It is safe to say that many people learn the dances of their culture before the language. Pictured are elementary school students learning how to dance by imitating their parents, holding hands and moving to the beat of the music. When the music is on a fast beat, good luck getting a spot in the line dance! Pictured is a wedding reception at Shenandoah Manor in 1993. (Author's collection.)

CHALDEAN RYDER CUP. In the Chaldean Golf League, the match was the old and the not-too-old against the young. Some described it as the "young and powerful" against the "slightly gray and experienced older men." The Chaldean Ryder Cup was held on July 6 and 7, 2001, and the trophy (and bragging rights) went to the young guys. Despite all the challenges, both had a great time building new friendships and lifelong memories. (Courtesy of Johnny Karmo.)

Senior players of the Shenandoah CIAAM League who played in the 2001 Chaldean RYDER CUP

Junior players of the Shenandoah CIAAM League who won the 2001 Chaldean RYDER CUP

WEST BLOOMFIELD'S ONLY GOLF COURSE. CIAAM has spent far more money on golf course capital improvement (not including the upkeep and general maintenance) than the $4.2 million cost to purchase the 18-hole course in 1989. The price for Chaldeans to learn the game of golf has been well worth it. Shenandoah is a public golf course and has been a place for enjoyment for Chaldeans and non-Chaldeans, members and nonmembers, since its acquisition by CIAAM. The 145 acres include a brand new pro shop, dining, and a rebuilt facility to house and maintain all golf and greens equipment for the enjoyment of golfers and their guests. (Courtesy of Faris Nalu.)

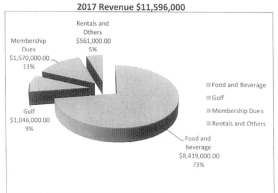

2017 Revenue $11,596,000

- Membership Dues $1,570,000.00 — 13%
- Rentals and Others $561,000.00 — 5%
- Golf $1,046,000.00 — 9%
- Food and Beverage $8,419,000.00 — 73%

Legend:
- Food and Beverage
- Golf
- Membership Dues
- Rentals and Others

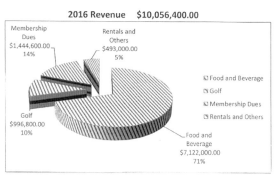

2016 Revenue $10,056,400.00

- Membership Dues $1,444,600.00 — 14%
- Rentals and Others $493,000.00 — 5%
- Golf $996,800.00 — 10%
- Food and Beverage $7,122,000.00 — 71%

Legend:
- Food and Beverage
- Golf
- Membership Dues
- Rentals and Others

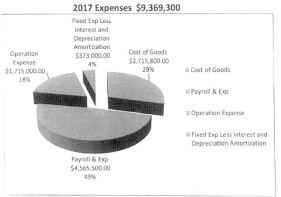

2017 Expenses $9,369,300

- Fixed Exp Less interest and Depreciation Amortization $373,000.00 — 4%
- Cost of Goods $2,715,800.00 — 29%
- Operation Expense $1,715,000.00 — 18%
- Payroll & Exp $4,565,500.00 — 49%

Legend:
- Cost of Goods
- Payroll & Exp
- Operation Expense
- Fixed Exp Less interest and Depreciation Amortization

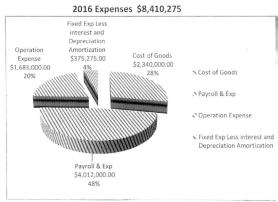

2016 Expenses $8,410,275

- Fixed Exp Less interest and Depreciation Amortization $375,275.00 — 4%
- Cost of Goods $2,340,000.00 — 28%
- Operation Expense $1,683,000.00 — 20%
- Payroll & Exp $4,012,000.00 — 48%

Legend:
- Cost of Goods
- Payroll & Exp
- Operation Expense
- Fixed Exp Less interest and Depreciation Amortization

Shenandoah Report Card. On or before the end of each year, the CIAAM president is required to report to the general members of the association about general business and affairs, club financial conditions, and future planning at a general membership meeting, which is typically scheduled in November or December. Shenandoah Country Club's fiscal year corresponds with the calendar year. Pictured here are reports on Shenandoah's performance for fiscal year 2016 (above) and 2017 (below). Club performance is subject to various factors, such as overall economic conditions, membership activity, and the general manager's skills and banquet experience. The general membership meeting explanation and comparison and past performance is not a guarantee of future results. (Courtesy of CIAAM files and records.)

SOMETHING FOR EVERYONE. For kids, Shenandoah has a pool, gym, and golf lessons. For teenagers, there is basketball, volleyball, and golf. Those in their 20s and 30s enjoy all the above plus poker, backgammon, and everything else in the 90,000-square-foot building and 18-hole golf course. The older set gets together with friends to play games of wishliani, *concan*, and maybe *tawlee*, where the loser pays the food bill. (Both, author's collection.)

RELAX AND ENJOY. For many regulars, "club day" is Tuesday, though no one knows why. It is the day when members catch up on the latest news and sports while enjoying a drink or cigar, followed by Middle Eastern cold and hot appetizers and a favorite entree or the chef's special of the day. Seen here is a group of friends on the lower-level terrace, adjacent to the members' private cigar lounge. (Author's collection.)

MESOPOTAMIA'S OLDEST BOARD GAME. Backgammon is a game that depends on equal measures of skill, strategy, and luck. It is the world's oldest board game, dating to 3000 BC in Mesopotamia. A great number of club members like to challenge each other to a game or two. Shenandoah hosts a backgammon tournament annually. (Author's collection.)

Seven

The Club's Impact

Influence on Chaldeans and US Society

As the famous saying goes, all roads lead to Rome. For the Chaldean community of Michigan, instead of Rome, all roads lead to CIAAM.

The CIAAM board and club members are a positive reflection of the community in the United States. In every image in this chapter, the people, places, and events are well connected to CIAAM board members.

In the 1930s and 1940s, a small group of Chaldean men met many times to discuss forming a club. When they finally elected the first board of 12 members on April 24, 1943, this marked the birth of CIA, the Chaldean Iraqi Association.

One of the most urgent goals was bringing an Aramaic-speaking priest to Detroit. This was achieved when Fr. Thomas Bidawid arrived in Detroit on February 24, 1947. There was also a Chaldean community in Mexico, but it never got an Aramaic-speaking priest, and no Chaldean church was ever built in Mexico. As a result, the Chaldean community there was lost.

As that very first board illustrates, CIAAM members have an ethical and moral responsibility to be an active and effective voice in the area where they live and work. The CIAAM organization has a long history of experience, qualifications, and credibility to play a critical role in the community's political action and involvement in its new country. It is a strong belief of the club that each and every member is a Chaldean ambassador who represents the Chaldean identity to the outside community.

ROYAL VISIT. The last king of Iraq, Faisal II, traveled to the United States on an informal, unofficial five-week tour in 1952. He arrived by plane at Willow Run Airport at 8:00 p.m. on August 18 and was greeted by leaders of the Chaldean community. As the *Detroit Free Press* reported the next day, "Thomas (Tobia) J. Hakim, Joe Acho and Jack Najor are the co-chairmen of the reception arranged by the Chaldean Iraqi organization of Detroit," referring to the Chaldean Iraqi Association. The reception team also included Salim Sarafa, Joe Najor, and Fr. Thomas Rais, the pastor of Mother of God. The king spent the night at the Dearborn Inn. The next day, the royal party toured the Ford Tank and Rouge plants and had lunch with Ford officials. (Courtesy of Tobia Hakim Archives.)

UNITY WITH THE CHURCH. Mother of God Chaldean Catholic Church has been a unifying factor in the community since the arrival of the first priest in Detroit in 1947. Many changes took place regarding basic matters of faith. One of them was using the liturgical language of Aramaic in its Chaldean dialect in the Aramaic Mass, which strengthened people's sense of belonging to their church and community. (Courtesy of Salim Kas-Shamoun.)

A Date with the President. The Chaldean community in America has been invited by many Iraqi presidents to visit their homeland. Gen. Abdul Karim Kassem, the most powerful man after the 1958 revolution that changed Iraq from a kingdom to a republic, asked the visiting Chaldean delegation to be proud of their roots and to remain good ambassadors to their country of birth. He was known to treat the Christians in Iraq as equal citizens. The tradition of visiting the homeland continued during the reign of Saddam Hussein. (Courtesy of Eddie Bacall.)

A Call for Unity. Assyrians began immigrating to the United States after World War I after many failed attempts to build a self-governing nation in their homeland, the Hakkari area (north of Iraq and south of Turkey). They were exposed to deportation, kidnapping, and embezzlement. The vivid memory of the 1933 Simele massacre of Assyrians by the government in northern Iraq will be in the minds and hearts of generations to come. Shown in the late 1970s, Chaldean clergy from Detroit, including Fr. Michael Bazzi (far left), Fr. George Garmo (second from left), and Fr. Sarhad Jammo (fourth from right), were joined by activist Afram D. Rayis (second from right) and *Al-Mashriq* newspaper publisher Napoleon Bashi (far right), who worked to find common ground between the two communities. (Courtesy of Samir and Bernadet Bashi.)

PATH TO SUCCESS. All 12 members of the original board of 1943 owned stores except for Daoud Kory, who was a bar owner and operator. The corner stores were a perfect fit and an economically viable business for newcomers who had very limited education and hardly spoke English. As more Chaldean youth have entered the professional fields, retail is no longer a major family business that passes from one generation to the next. (Courtesy of Chaldean Cultural Center.)

JOINT EFFORTS. On September 1, 1989, the Chaldean American Political Action Committee (CAPAC) held a fundraising event at Southfield Manor for a prominent member of the Detroit police force, Commander Gil Hill, in support of his election as a Detroit city councilman. Commander Hill is also remembered from the movie *Beverly Hills Cop* with Eddie Murphy. (Courtesy of Jason Jarjosa.)

A GRAND TIME. On June 3, 1989, CIAM members were invited to the governor's reception at the Grand Hotel on Mackinac Island as part of the Greater Detroit Chamber of Commerce's ninth annual legislative conference. The objective was to encourage people from the private and public sectors to participate in business issues. From left to right are Tarik Daoud of Al Long Ford; Nabby Yono of the Associated Food Dealers (AFD) board; Richard Gergis, AFD political action committee; Ed McNamara, Wayne County executive; Rick Przebieda, Paddington Corporation district manager; Mike George, CIAM president and Melody Farms owner; Sam Yono, AFD chairman; Joe Sarafa, AFD executive director; Barbara Manlove, AFD board; and Clyde Cleveland, J&B Scotch state manager and Detroit city councilman. (Courtesy of Nabby Yono.)

WORKING TOGETHER. The dominance of the grocery store business has in a large part contributed to the strength of the community ties today, according to Dr. Mary Sengstock, professor of sociology at Wayne State University. The Chaldean community illustrates how a dominant occupation can help mold a strong ethnic community. This photograph illustrates the opportunity for Chaldeans and Detroit business leaders to work together to revive the city's business environment. (Courtesy of Nabby Yono.)

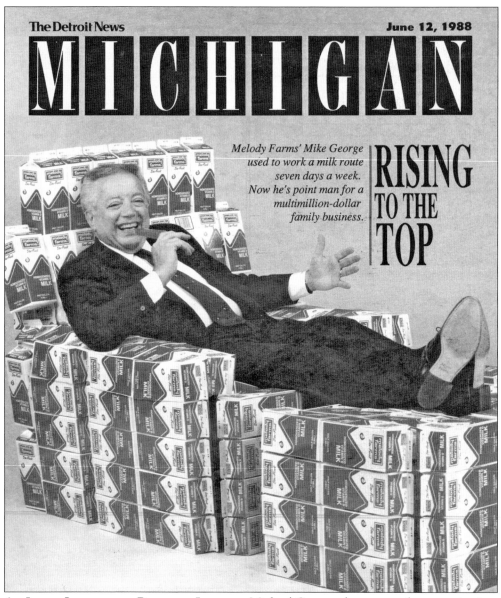

An Iconic Leader with Powerful Insights. Michael George, the master of communication, was the proud son of a Mesopotamian immigrant who reached the pinnacle of every immigrant's dream by owning his own business, the Melody Farms dairy company. Raised with strong family ethics in the Christian faith, Mike George was instrumental in building the club the way it was, rather than just another place for Middle Eastern and Chaldean food or an enhanced chai-khana. He changed the way the community gathered, as well as everything in the proposed site plans of Southfield Manor—the size, the layout, the function, and most importantly, the clients. Rather than a gathering place for men only, as is the case with the Chaldean club in San Diego, "We are building the club with the entire family in mind," said George at the construction meeting in 1979. (Courtesy of the *Detroit News*.)

GATHERING SPOT. Mother of God Church in Southfield was built with a basement in mind, just like the first and second Mother of God Church buildings, which were both in Detroit and on the same street, Hamilton Avenue. The church used the basement to host religious classes for various ages, as well as youth groups, choir practice, and other community activities. With the construction of the new club building, the heart of the action shifted just west of the church parking lot to Southfield Manor, but the church remains a spiritual home for all Chaldeans. (Both, author's collection.)

CULTURAL ADAPTATIONS AND INFLUENCE. A group of friends, business associates, engineers, surveyors, bankers and real estate developers took the time to enjoy one of America's most popular games, baseball. The younger generation joined with their fathers and uncles to watch the game and learn about each other's family, history, and culture, and of course, support the hometown team. It is truly a representation of the American melting pot, where different nationalities and cultures are united as Americans. (Courtesy of Mel Joseph, Kem-Tec Professional Engineers and Surveyors.)

BUILDING BRIDGES. In July 2002, CIAAM invited the Arab American Democratic Caucus to the Chaldean guest house at Southfield Manor. A special guest, Michigan Democratic Party chairman Mark Brewer, joined the attendees to build bridges between the Arab and Chaldean communities and the Democratic Party in Michigan. Jacob Bacall, CIAAM president at the time, extended his gratitude for Brewer's assistance in securing grants for the Chaldean Cultural Center, which is housed in Shenandoah Country Club. (Author's collection.)

TREASURE FROM THE ROYAL TOMBS OF UR. On April 25, 2001, Chaldeans from various organizations, including CIAAM, joined leaders from the Jewish Community Center (JCC) to visit a Detroit Institute of Arts exhibit, Treasures from the Royal Tombs of Ur. Fr. Sarhad Jammo, vicar general of the Chaldean Diocese of the United States; Rabbi Marla Feldman of JCC; and Kathy Krans, Michigan Board of Education president, were on hand. Leaders from both communities emphasized further fostering the working relationship, common interests, and joint programs in all areas. (Courtesy of *Chaldean Detroit Times*.)

Chaldean Detroit Times page 2

Chaldean Federation of America

ܣܝܡܐ ܕܚܘܝܕܐ ܕܟܠܕܝܐ ܕܐܡܪܝܟܐ

الاتحـاد الكلـداني الامـريكي

Joint Visit of the Chaldean Federation of America and the Jewish Community Council to UR Exhibit

On April 25, 2001, about 50 leaders from the CFA and JCC met and exchanged friendly remarks and views of working relationship between the two communities on a joint visit to DIA Exhibit " Treasurers from the Royal Tombs of Ur".

Fr. Dr. Sarhad Jammo, Vicar General of the Chaldean Diocese of USA, Rabbi Marla Feldman of JCC and Ms. Kathy Krans, president of the state of Michigan Board of Education, were on hand at the event.

In his remarks, Mr. Saad Marouf, the newly elected chairman of the CFA commende the efforts of DIA and JCC to co-sponsor this tour with the CFA and emphasized on the importance to further foster the working relationship between the two communities for what is good and common interest and encouraged joint programs i all areas.

EVERY IMMIGRANT'S DREAM. The hospitality business is becoming the new trade of Chaldeans in Metro Detroit. For many Chaldeans who operate their hotel business in many states, it serves as an opportunity for cultural adaptation. Everyone is living their own American dream. Most of the Chaldean men pictured here are new hotel owners. From left to right are (first row) Dia Shammami, Mark Karmo, Eddie Savaya, Aboud Kasgorgis, Hanna Shina, Masoud Kasgorgis, Jason Bacall, Majid Dado, Farook Kenaya, Sabah Abdal, Maher Abdulnoor, Steve Karmo, Jalal Yatooma, and Amir Kuza; (second row) Tony Konja, Keith Shunia, David Kalasho, Donny Jarbo, Mike Bacall, Nabil Cholagh, Saber Kassab, Tom Kato, Naseer Rayes, Fawzi Delli, Duraid Rayis, Walid Gulli, Atheer Yaldo, Hani Yatooma, Saher Abdulnoor, and Kays Sweis. (Courtesy of Mike Bacall.)

OUR PRIEST, OUR BISHOP. "Now I carry you in my heart whenever I celebrate Mass," said Bishop Francis Kalabat in his homily at his ordination at Mother of God Church on June 14, 2014. "Father Frank" was born on May 13, 1970, and ordained a priest in 1995. "We are confident that God will do many great things through him and will strengthen him as a good shepherd," said Archbishop Allen H. Vigneron of Detroit. Well-wishers began lining up at 5:00 a.m. to attend the historic event. (Author's collection.)

ROME WITH LOVE. With more than 60 members in attendance, CIAAM was well represented at the installation ceremony of His Beatitude Mar Emmanuel III Delly, Chaldean patriarch of Babylon, on November 24, 2007. He was the first Chaldean cardinal installed by Pope Benedict XVI. During the ceremony, the pope placed the red hat (*biretta*) on the head of Cardinal Delly, executing the rituals of the Oriental Chaldean Church. (Author's collection.)

A Premier Visit. During his two-day visit to Michigan in 2005, Iraqi prime minister Ibrahim al-Jaafari met and listened to the issues and concerns of a large group from the Iraqi community at Shenandoah Country Club. Most echoed the same question: "What are you, as the most powerful figure in the government, going to do to protect the remaining Christians of Iraq, their villages, property, and lifelong savings, from the hands of terrorists?" His answer was diplomatic and soothing, but not healing. (Author's collection.)

Preserving Syriac Culture. From June 21 to 24, 2015, ongoing efforts to preserve Syriac and neo-Aramaic cultural heritage were furthered at the seventh annual Syriac Symposium at the Catholic University of America in Washington, DC. Dr. Robin Darling Young (seated at left) was the chair and organizer of the forum. Speakers from all over the continent had the chance to speak and exchange ideas. Bishop Francis Kalabat and Bishop Saad Sirop were both present to lead the efforts to preserve Syriac heritage through a collection of interviews and recordings. (Author's collection.)

VOICE OF THE CHALDEANS. *The Chaldean Voice* was founded in North America in the early 1980s. Bishop Ibrahim Ibrahim strengthened the voice of the Chaldeans to the world with his support. The independent radio station broadcasts out of Southfield on 690 AM and is heard all over the world. *The Chaldean Voice* has been produced and directed by volunteers for nearly 40 years, including Shoki Konja, Diha Babi, Fawzi Delli, Saher Yaldo, Janan Sinawi, Saher Haddad, and the late Intisar Yono. (Courtesy of Saher Yaldo.)

A PAGE FROM HISTORY. *Chaldeans in Detroit*, the author's first book, tells the story of a small group of people who left their hilltop village of Telkaif, Iraq, and found their way to Detroit at the beginning of the 20th century. It documents their long journey to the American dream. The book was published in December 2014 by Arcadia Publishing as part of its Images of America series. Pictured at the book launch party on December 16, 2014, at Shenandoah Country Club are architect Victor Saroki, Jamal Kallabat, and Derek Dickow. Samira Yako Cholagh appears in the background. (Courtesy of Saher Yaldo.)

Eight

OUR IDENTITY
PEOPLE'S REFLECTION

A century ago, Chaldeans came primarily from humble beginnings and simple agricultural villages, weathered difficult times and insurmountable odds in Iraq, and adopted a new country, America. They left behind poverty, illiteracy, and financial hardship to enjoy prosperity and freedom by immigrating to this great country of the United States of America. The pioneers achieved their triumph by taking it upon themselves to sacrifice for others to enjoy life in peace and harmony in the truly diverse culture of the melting pot.

The histories of the Polish, Irish, German, and Anglo-Saxon immigrants show amazing similarities. They also arrived here as farmers to join the Industrial Revolution. As the Chaldean community continues to assimilate into the American mainstream, its contributions to society have grown tremendously through thousands of businesses and professions.

Attitude determines altitude, and the community's vision is focused on value-oriented, compassionate, ethical, and socially responsible people. The community's dream is to have a real-world society made of community leaders and world citizens. Exchanging culture is always a two-way street. This chapter is a reflection of people, Chaldeans and non-Chaldeans, interacting with one another.

LONG LIVE HIS MAJESTY. In 1952, the Iraqi community of Detroit gave a reception in honor of King Faisal II Al-Hashimi of Iraq and Prince Abdul-Ilah, regent of Iraq. While five-year-old Patricia Hakim presented King Faisal with a huge bouquet of white roses, the spectators, mostly of Iraqi descent, shouted in Arabic, "long live his majesty!" (Courtesy of Tobia Hakim archives.)

UNITED UNDER ONE GOD. "I would hope and believe this Chaldean cultural center will help us understand our friends in ways we have not in the past," said Rev. Jack Freed. Reverend Freed has been a thread in weaving the many faiths and cultures of the West Bloomfield area into a dynamic tapestry. (Author's collection.)

THE CHALDEANS OF DETROIT. In 1973, Detroit for the first time had more black than white residents. Voters elected the first black mayor, Coleman A. Young, a charismatic civil rights leader. The Chaldean community was a big supporter of Mayor Young. "I love the Chaldean people; I love their work ethic. Their grocery stores and businesses are great assets to the city," said the newly elected mayor. From left to right are Joe Shaya, Judge Damon Keith, Mayor Young, and two unidentified. (Courtesy of Linda Shaya.)

LOVE AND SUPPORT. The Chaldean Iraqi American Association of Michigan always took a leading role in building bridges with other community programs and leaders, including the NAACP, and also hosting many fundraising events for local and state politicians through the years. "I appreciate the support and friendship of the Chaldean community very much. Your contribution to the city is immeasurable," said Dennis Archer, mayor of Detroit (center), in 1997 at Southfield Manor. Archer is pictured with Isam Yaldo (left) and Edward Yaldo. (Courtesy of CIAAM files and records.)

SPECIAL REPORT

The Detroit News

Civilization's cracked cradle

Bloody purges, religious strife mark history of modern Iraq

Saddam Hussein mires Iraq in war

Since Saddam Hussein became Iraq's undisputed leader, the nation has suffered through a series of wars. First, he launched an indecisive eight-year war with Iran that cost thousands of lives. His invasion of Kuwait, which prompted a war by the United States and a coalition of forces, cost Iraq an estimated 100,000 soldiers and a retreat from Kuwait. Since that surrender, Saddam's Iraq has suffered under economic sanctions and restrictions on its airspace.

GEOGRAPHY/REGION
Mostly broad plains; marshland in the southeast; mountains along borders with Iran and Turkey.

Mountains
Foothills
Tigris/
Euphrates delta
Western/
southern desert

2002 POPULATION (in millions)
Iraq 24
U.S. 288

DISTANCE FROM DETROIT TO BAGHDAD: 6,258 miles

TURKEY
Michigan
Iraq
Mosul
Tel Kaif
NORTHERN NO-FLY ZONE
SYRIA
Anah
Al Qa'im
Samarra
Tharthar Lake
IRAQ
Ar Rutbah
50 MILES
Baghdad
JORDAN
Habbaniyah Lake
SOUTHERN NO-FLY ZONE
Badrah
IRAN
Razzaza Lake
Karbala
Nukhayb
An Najaf
As Samawah
Al Amarah
SAUDI ARABIA
IRAQ
MICHIGAN
As Salman
Hammar Lake
Al Basrah
KUWAIT

Key Groups

Kurdish
The Kurds make up the largest ethnic minority in Iraq, as well as minorities in neighboring Turkey, Armenia and Iran. Since the end of World War I, Kurdish activists have been trying to set up a Kurdish state in the region.

Sunni Muslim
The vast majority of Muslims across the world, and most Arabs, follow this sect of Islam. In Iraq, Sunni Muslims make up only about 20 percent of the population, but Saddam Hussein is a Sunni, as are most of his key government officials.

Shi'ite Muslim
About 60 percent of Iraq's population is Shi'ite, though this religious group has never held power in the country. Saddam Hussein has had to suppress Shi'ite uprisings during his rule, and Shi'ite assassins have tried to kill him.

By Cameron McWhirter
The Detroit News

The volume of rhetoric increases daily in Washington, D.C., for the overthrow of the resilient dictatorship of Saddam Hussein, which has survived a brutal defeat by the United States and its allies in 1991 and 11 subsequent years of strict economic sanctions.

But for all the martial chatter, the complicated history of Iraq, set in the heart of the combustible Middle East, still is poorly understood by most Americans.

The story of modern Iraq is a bloody one, forged by diplomatic intrigue, layered in religious and cultural divisions, plagued by brutal regimes and fed by billions of dollars gained from the country's one extremely profitable export: oil.

Most scholars agree that modern Iraq began with the British. Before World War I, the Ottoman Empire controlled the area and much of the Middle East. But the Turks joined the Germans on the losing side of that war — and the British with their Arab allies captured much of the land. They then created colonies and quasi-independent countries.

The British set up Iraq as a protectorate that allowed British military bases. They also thought the area might have oil.

"The only reason there is an Iraq today is because Britain willed it," says Rashid Khalidi, a professor of Middle Eastern history at the University of Chicago.

"The question has always been: What is the polity of Iraq? What is

Life expectancy (in years)	Languages	ECONOMY		GDP (2000 est. in U.S. dollars)		RELIGION	ETHNIC GROUPS
Iraq 67	Arabic	Crude oil reserves: 113 billion barrels		Iraq $57 billion		Shi'ite Muslim / Sunni Muslim	Arab 75%–80%
U.S. 77	Kurdish	Ranks No. 2 behind Saudi Arabia, which has 262 billion barrels in reserve.		U.S. $9.96 trillion			Kurd 15%–20%
	Assyrian	**Industries**	**Agricultural products**	Per capita GDP (2000 est. in U.S. dollars)		60% 35%	Turkmen, Assyrian and others
Literacy[1]	Armenian	Oil	Wheat Cotton	Iraq $2,500			Less than 5%
58% of Iraq's population is literate.		Natural gas	Barley Dates	U.S. $36,200		Christian 5%	
Male 71%		Phosphates	Rice Poultry			(Jewish and Yazidi less than 1%)	
Female 45%		Sulfur	Tobacco				

1 — 1995 estimate.

Iraq: 168,751 square miles
Michigan: 96,810 square miles

Source: Detroit news research and Gannett News Service

The Detroit News

CHALDEAN POPULATION IN MICHIGAN. Today, some 175,000 to 200,000 Chaldeans, who are Eastern Rite Catholic, led by the patriarch of Babylon, and affiliated with the Roman Catholic Church, are in the United States. Metro Detroit, 6,258 miles from Baghdad, is thought to host the largest population of Chaldeans in the world. Telkaif, the birthplace of the early Christian pioneers, can be seen on this map of Iraq. There are more Chaldeans in the greater Detroit area than in Baghdad, Mosul, and Basra combined, and it is thought that the Chaldean population in Michigan has exceeded that in Iraq, historically the land of Ur or Mesopotamia. Thousands of years later, the name Mesopotamia is long gone. (Author's collection.)

A TRIBAL WELCOME. Ghazi al-Yawer, newly appointed president under the Iraqi interim government from 2004 to 2005, visited Washington in June 2004 and met a large group of Iraqi Americans who immigrated within the past five decades. CIAAM was heavily represented. After a short speech, Sheikh al-Yawer, pictured in his tribal robes, asked, "is there anyone here from Detroit with the last name Sesi?" The family of the late Abdel Karim Sesi were not present, but al-Yawer explained how Sesi, a Christian from Telkaif, was very influential to al-Yawer's grandfather and served as a financial advisor and teacher to the sheikh's children, including Ghazi. He wanted to offer the Sesi family "more than a word of thanks." (Author's collection.)

DIVERSE CULTURE. A diverse community is what Michigan is all about. Members of CIAAM use the Shenandoah Club as their community guesthouse when different cultures come together as one community living side by side as Americans. Here, individuals with different religions, cultures, and professions get together to break bread in Shenandoah's private dining room in 2016. Among them are former US district judge Gerald E. Rosen, who is Jewish; Michigan Supreme Court justice Kurt T. Wilder, who is African American; and Osama Siblani, Muslim and long-serving editor and publisher of *Sada Al Watan*. The luncheon was hosted by their friends in the Chaldean community, the Catholic Bacall brothers. (Author's collection.)

Lost in Translation. Growing up in New Jersey, Joyce Wiswell had never heard of Chaldeans. At her job interview at the *Chaldean News* in 2004, she asked, "So what exactly are Chaldeans?" She was hired and spent more than 12 years at the magazine. "My family never did get the hang of the community, though," she said. "Driving home from work, I frequently called my mother, Elaine, to say hello. One of her first questions was always: 'How are the Caledonians?' " (Courtesy of Joyce Wiswell.)

"I Know Chaldeans Well." On May 31, 2017, a small group from St. Thomas Chaldean Church met Pope Francis at St. Peter's Square. He met face-to-face with his audience, including an active young seminarian, Junior Jwad, and John Zia Oram, who has a well-known radio program in metro Detroit. They had a few special gifts for the pope, among them a book about Chaldeans in Detroit. "Your Holiness, this is a book about Chaldeans in America," began Oram. But before he could get another word out, Pope Francis chuckled. "Of course, I know Chaldeans well!" he exclaimed. Oram is seen during this memorable experience. (Courtesy of John Zia Oram.)

Nine

Chaldean Cultural Center

The History of the People of the Past

The idea for the Chaldean Cultural Center (CCC) began with the pioneers of CIA in the late 1930s and early 1940s. On August 31, 1965, articles of organization were filed by Salim Sarafa, the association president at the time. It was not possible to build a museum at the first home of CIAAM, Southfield Manor, but the purchase of Shenandoah made the idea of a museum realistic.

The new Shenandoah Country Club plans included an area near the main entrance to house the long-awaited community center. The formation of the CCC board of directors served as a light at the end of the tunnel. A nonprofit 501(c)(3) was created, and the real work of building a museum finally began. The New York architectural firm of Saylor+Sirola was selected to design the museum. Sanan Media, which is also New York–based, was selected to handle all the media. LifeFormations, located in Ohio, was hired to build the museum. All three consultants finalized the exhibits for each gallery.

During the early years of research, members of the CCC met with the staff of other institutions to learn the details of putting together a cultural center. Some of the organizations consulted included the Detroit Institute of Arts, the Detroit Historical Society, the Arab American National Museum, the Museum of African American History, and the Holocaust Memorial Center. Early on, the CCC board of directors decided that the museum would be sophisticated, professional, and have state-of-the-art exhibits and media.

Between 2003 and 2005, exhibition themes for the museum were chosen. There would be five galleries: Chaldeans in the Ancient World, Faith and Church, Village Life, Journey to America, and Chaldeans Today. It should be noted that the museum was to be the primary function of the CCC, but not the only one. The center was to also develop programming, be an educational and research facility, be the archivist for the Chaldean community, and provide other appropriate services.

In July 2005, Country Fresh Dairy, the largest dairy company in Michigan, took the lead in donating one percent of all its sales (including ice cream) sold by Chaldean merchants. A revenue of about $100,000 annually was secured, and additional funding was raised through other sources.

Over 5,000 years of history is being told, and that is just the beginning of the story, since the Chaldeans are still a vibrant and thriving community. The museum officially opened to the public on May 2, 2017.

GRAND ENTRANCE. King Nebuchadnezzar II ruled the Neo-Babylonian Empire, also known as the Chaldean Empire, from 605 to 562 BC. He built the Processional Way and the Ishtar Gate, which led into the inner city of Babylon. The gate was dedicated to the Babylonian goddess Ishtar, who represented fertility, love, and war. In the foreground is an authentic replica of Hammurabi's Stele, purchased from the Louvre. The interactive display next to the stele identifies some of the 282 laws that are written on it in cuneiform along with their English translations. (Both, courtesy of Chaldean Cultural Center.)

THE START OF IT ALL. As early as 3500 BC, in the fertile land between the Tigris and Euphrates Rivers, the first true cities developed in southern Mesopotamia. The rich soil produced crops of wheat and other grains, a sophisticated irrigation system was developed, and the people fished and farmed at the confluence of the rivers. Eventually, these cities developed a central ruling authority and began trading with other areas to obtain needed and desired goods. Under the diorama is a case with artifacts including a cylinder seal and a clay tablet. There is also a reader rail that gives a timeline of major events in Mesopotamian history. (Courtesy of Chaldean Cultural Center.)

CONTRIBUTIONS OF A LIFETIME. This interactive exhibit contains narratives depicting different Babylonian achievements, including descriptions of the Processional Way and Ishtar Gate; the earliest known map of the world (sixth century BC) showing Babylon as the geographic center; a math tablet using the sexagesimal system (counting in 60s); a medical tablet featuring prescriptions for specific ailments; and an astronomical tablet that brought predictability to the calendar based on the movement of the moon. (Courtesy of Chaldean Cultural Center.)

THE TIME OF CHRIST, 33 AD. Artifacts and images tell the story of how the Chaldeans were converted to Christianity by St. Thomas the Apostle and his followers, Mar Addai and Mar Mari. In the center is a replica of the baptismal font from St. Peter's Church in Mosul, Iraq. (Courtesy of Chaldean Cultural Center.)

THE MOTHER OF GOD. This mosaic in the Faith and Church Gallery is an illuminated icon of Theotokos and Child based on a mosaic in the Hagia Sophia in Istanbul, Turkey. *Theotokos* is a Greek word meaning "God-bearer." The Council of Ephesus decreed in 431 that Mary is Theotokos because her son, Jesus, is both God and man: one person with two natures (divine and human) intimately and hypostatically united. (Courtesy of Chaldean Cultural Center.)

THIS FOR THAT. Although this life-size figure of a Chaldean man in authentic clothing is standing in a wheat field with farming tools next to him, the farmer is dressed to go to another village to barter. In front of him is a *bukcha* or bundle that holds various pieces of adult and children's clothing, linens, and other items to exchange for goods that he needs. (Courtesy of Chaldean Cultural Center.)

MOTHER'S HARD-WORKING HANDS. In the Village Gallery, there is a life-size figure of a Chaldean woman in authentic clothing making bread in her courtyard. She is using a *khwana* for rolling out the dough, and near her is the *tanoor* or clay oven for baking the bread. It was the woman's responsibility to take care of the home, cook, and raise the young children. (Courtesy of Chaldean Cultural Center.)

YOUR FRIENDLY NEIGHBORHOOD STORE. In the Journey Gallery, there is a recreation of a 1930s Chaldean-owned Detroit grocery store. This is an immersive environment; the visitor is inside the store looking through the window onto Woodward Avenue. The shelves hold reproductions of boxes, bottles, and canned goods available at that time. A vintage radio broadcasts a Tigers baseball game from that era. The cash register, adding machine, and signs are authentic to the 1930s. (Courtesy of Chaldean Cultural Center.)

CONTRIBUTING TO AMERICA'S MOSAIC. In the Today Gallery, there is a photo exhibit of 20 pioneers, titled Our Past. They were among the first to come to America and make it their permanent home. This exhibit is meant to honor all those who ventured to a new country, not necessarily knowing the language but willing to assimilate into American society while not losing their Chaldean identity. They established their families here and became entrepreneurs in Detroit's economic sector. (Courtesy of Chaldean Cultural Center.)

GRAND ENTRANCE. At the main entrance to the museum exhibition, one finds oneself in front of a large door that gives a sense of dignity, wonder, and timelessness. It is the modern counterpart to the great portals that were the traditional gateways to ancient walled cities. Standing in front of the gate is Kaya Sanan, founder of New York–based Sanan Media, who was selected to handle all the media. (Author's collection.)

BLESSING FROM ABOVE. On Tuesday, April 25, 2017, a small group of volunteers, donors, and honorary sponsors marked the soft launch of the CCC museum, housed inside SCC in West Bloomfield. As the prayer ceremony began, three bishops of the Chaldean church led the guests to the museum. Holy water was sprinkled for a special blessing. (Courtesy of Chaldean Cultural Center.)

An Exciting Evening. This photograph, taken at the CCC grand opening on September 13, 2017, shows a woman baking bread and illustrates how women who followed the traditional role as homemakers often cooked, cleaned, and helped with household chores and raised their children. They were the heart and nurturers of the family. Chaldean families quickly adapted from the hard struggle of village life to a modern life in America. The five-gallery museum tells their story along with who Chaldeans are, where they came from, and why they chose Detroit to be the capital of the Chaldeans in the United States. (Courtesy of Judy Sarafa Jonna.)

BIBLIOGRAPHY

Bacall, Jacob. *Chaldeans in Detroit*. Charleston, SC: Arcadia Publishing, 2014.

Bak, Richard. *The Story of Ethnic Detroit: Metropolitan Detroit Guest Guide*. Royal Oak, MI: Hour Media LLC, 2001.

Bazzi, Fr. Michael. *Tilkepe: Past and Present*. Mosul, Iraq: Gumhuria Printing (Arabic Edition), 1969 and 1991.

Chaldean American Ladies of Charity. *Ma Baseema*. Ann Arbor, MI: Huron River Press, 2010.

The Chaldean News, November 2017.

Dabish, Sam (Shamoun). *The History of the Iraqi Community in America*. Baghdad, Iraq: The Iraqi Printing Press (Arabic Edition), 1975.

DBusiness II, issue 2 (2016).

The Michigan Catholic, September 12, 1980.

Munier, Gilles. *Iraq: An Illustrated History and Guide*. Northampton, MA: Interlink Publishing Group Inc., 2004.

Nasrallah, Nawal. *Delights from the Garden of Eden*. Bloomington, IN: 1st Books Library/Author House Publishing, 2004.

Perry, Bryon. *The Chaldeans*. Troy, MI: Tepel Brothers Printing Company, 2008.

Rassam, Suha. *Christianity in Iraq*. Herefordshire, UK: Action Publishing Technology Ltd., 2005.

Saroki-Sarafa, Josephine M. and Julia Najor-Hallahan. *The Chaldean American Community*. Oak Park, MI: Eastern Graphics and Printing, 1990.

Sengstock, Mary C. *Chaldeans in Michigan*. East Lansing, MI: Michigan State University Press, 2005.

Stephen, Louis J. *The Chaldean Directory*. Eastpointe, MI: Nu-Ad Inc., 1998 and 2007.

West Bloomfield Eccentric 123, number 89. April 27, 1996.

DISCOVER THOUSANDS OF LOCAL HISTORY BOOKS
FEATURING MILLIONS OF VINTAGE IMAGES

Arcadia Publishing, the leading local history publisher in the United States, is committed to making history accessible and meaningful through publishing books that celebrate and preserve the heritage of America's people and places.

Find more books like this at
www.arcadiapublishing.com

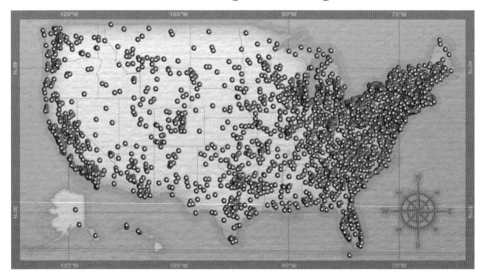

Search for your hometown history, your old stomping grounds, and even your favorite sports team.